Six Years to Sunrise

Karen Hoff Lafnear

Best Wishes — To Kurt and Anita. 8/19/00

Catherine Hoff Mount

Catherine Hoff Mount
Karen Hoff Lafnear

Co-Author: Harry Knitter

KORDENE PUBLICATIONS, LTD.
Clarkston, Michigan

Published by Kordene Publications, P.O. Box 636, Clarkston, MI 48347-0636

Publisher's Cataloging-in-Publication Data

Six Years to Sunrise / Catherine Hoff Mount, Karen Hoff Lafnear, Harry Knitter — Clarkston, Michigan: Kordene Publications, Ltd., © 2000
p. ill. cm.

ISBN 0-9652333-4-0

Co-Authors: Catherine Hoff Mount and Karen Hoff Lafnear, Clarkston, Michigan
Knitter, Harry W., Co-Author and Editor.

1. BIOGRAPHY 2. EUROPEAN HISTORY 3. ROMANCE

Printed in the United States of America

TABLE OF CONTENTS

FOREWORD

Our names are Catherine (Dossi) and Karen Hoff. In 1939, when we were seven and three years old, respectively, we moved with our Mom to Bergen, Norway, from Auburn Heights, a suburb of Detroit. She and Dad had decided to get a fresh start in life back in their native land and Dad was to join us in a few months after building a nest egg of money to get us back on our feet after the tough years of the Great Depression. However, because of the outbreak of World War II, it took six long years for us to live as a family again.

Through letters, postcards, greeting cards, and telegrams, our parents attempted to keep each other informed about their separate lives. Unfortunately, Mom did not save Dad's letters from the period of 1939 through 1941, so none of them can be included here. In addition, during the years when mail was prohibited from 1942 through May of 1945, Mom did not write Dad, though she occasionally was able to contact him with brief Red Cross messages. Dad, on the other hand, wrote many of his most compelling letters during this period. He tucked them away to be mailed later, after the war, since there was no way they could be sent or received in the interim. When the war ended, the post office in Bergen unloaded bag after bag of letters, cards, and parcels sent by our Dad.

In the late 1990s, Karen and I discovered the original handwritten letters in shoe boxes in a closet of our parents' home shortly after their passing. We began to translate some of the correspondence from Norwegian to English to enable some of our family members in the United States to view them. Then we decided to make a family album and began to translate additional letters.

Each translated personal message enticed us to keep on going, and we eventually translated about 250 letters and telegrams our parents had stored in shoe boxes for over 50 years. As we completed this work, Karen and I decided that the story might make an interesting magazine article or even, possibly, a book of some sort. We subsequently contacted our neighbor, author Harry Knitter, to help us write and publish it.

At the time we started to work on this book, we added a number of our own recollections going back to the early days of the twentieth century when our parents were growing up in Norway and concluding when we were all reunited after World War II. We are proud of the way our family faced diversity and overcame challenge after challenge, especially during the war years.

The process of translating our parents' words was not without emotion. Although we were only little girls during the six years our family was split on both sides of the ocean, we both remember the intense moments our parents experienced during those years of frustration, loneliness, and tension brought on by the war and amplified by our unusual family circumstances. Tears flowed freely many times while we were translating our parents' loving words for each other.

Today, our family continues to keep our "old country" traditions intact and to follow the example of our parents as succeeding generations pick up where Mom and Dad left off. In our challenging and often confusing world, the love we share as a family is a source of strength and continuity for all of us.

As we look back, it's also the main reason our family survived and grew even closer after the period of time chronicled in *Six Years to Sunrise*.

Catherine Hoff Mount and Karen Hoff Lafnear

INTRODUCTION

When I began to work on this book, I was convinced that the letters written by the parents of Catherine and Karen Hoff, the two principal characters, would provide the most substantive information for the story behind *Six Years to Sunrise*. But the letters weren't the most helpful contributors to the story line after all.

I discovered that the vivid recollections and reminiscences of Catherine and Karen, some 50-plus years after the fact, give the family's story its spark and bring the adventure to life. And, a video of their family celebrating Carl Hoff's 85th birthday gave me an instant impression of the Hoffs: fun-loving, warm, considerate, affectionate, outgoing, conservative—the kind of people you would want to specify as ideal next-door neighbors.

Once we began the project, my role became that of a listener and editor rather than author. Together with Catherine and Karen, who furnished rough text copy for several chapters, as well as the letters, pictures, and maps, I sorted through all of the reference material and organized the information in chronological order before entering any of it on the computer. It was the informal discussion time I spent with them that yielded the most interesting stories, descriptions, and characterizations.

Throughout the project, they clung steadfastly to precision in every detail, every fact, and every shred of information they shared with me. They were methodical in building the story step by step, taking great pains to ensure accuracy at every turn.

Because I have Parkinson's Disease, the project occasionally decelerated to a slow walk, but the flow of input from Catherine and Karen never really let up, so they were often several steps ahead of me. Without their encouragement and cooperative support, we might still be hassling about the correct spelling of "Rosenkrantztarnet" rather than looking at a finished book.

To provide a broad context for the translated letters written between 1939 and 1945, we divided the book into three parts and included a brief overview of the war at the beginning of each part. For easy recognition of the source of the letters, we italicized Olga's and set Carl's in bold face. The girls' letters are also italicized.

While there were substantial challenges to overcome during the course of the project, I believe the end result is a book that is pleasingly readable, precisely accurate, and tenderly reflective of the love that sustained the family throughout the years. It is, in every sense, a love story and a true story.

In the final analysis, what was actually achieved turned out to be much better than what I had originally envisioned. If only all writing experiences could conclude in that wonderful way.

Harry Knitter

ACKNOWLEDGEMENTS

We are grateful for the support provided by friends and members of our family, who were generous in their co-operation and encouragement as *Six Years to Sunrise* became a reality after years of preparatory work.

First, we want to thank our husbands, Clarence Mount and Jim Lafnear, who had less than our full attention while we spent countless hours at the keyboards of our computers or in meetings with one another and with Harry Knitter in the development of this book.

We sincerely appreciate the input provided by Chris Flessland, Chester Hansen, Einar and Walborg Hoff, Willy and Brit Hoff, Marith (Tuppen) Aavik, Arne and Signe Birkeland, Svein A. Birkeland, Teresa Birkeland, Tore and Inger Gjelsvik, Tore and Mossa Thomassen, Stanley Hoff, Jayne and William Bannister, and Steve Lafnear.

We are pleased to acknowledge the significant contributions of Nancy Knitter, who served as a researcher, counselor, referee, editor, facilitator, and friend throughout the project. We also thank Becky Chown, an invaluable editing resource, and Jim Rehlin of Rehlin Graphics, who designed the cover and handled all other art requirements so ably. Mr. Knitter also wishes to extend his appreciation to Professor Linda Peckham of Lansing Community College, who provided valuable support early in the history of Kordene Publications.

We are grateful to Jill Armentrout of *The Oakland Press* and to the professionals at WDIV-TV and WXYZ-TV in Detroit for helping us publicize the Hoff family story and *Six Years to Sunrise*. Special thanks go to Mary Ann Hupp, Carmen Harlan, and Devin Scillian of Channel 4, Sandy McFee of Channel 7, and the consummate professional, Emmy Award-winning Erik Smith, who told our story so sensitively.

As our parents would have said,

"Tusen Takk."

Catherine and Karen Hoff

DEDICATION

We lovingly dedicate this
book to the memory of our parents,
Olga and Carl Hoff,
as a fitting tribute to the love
they shared with us and the
entire family.

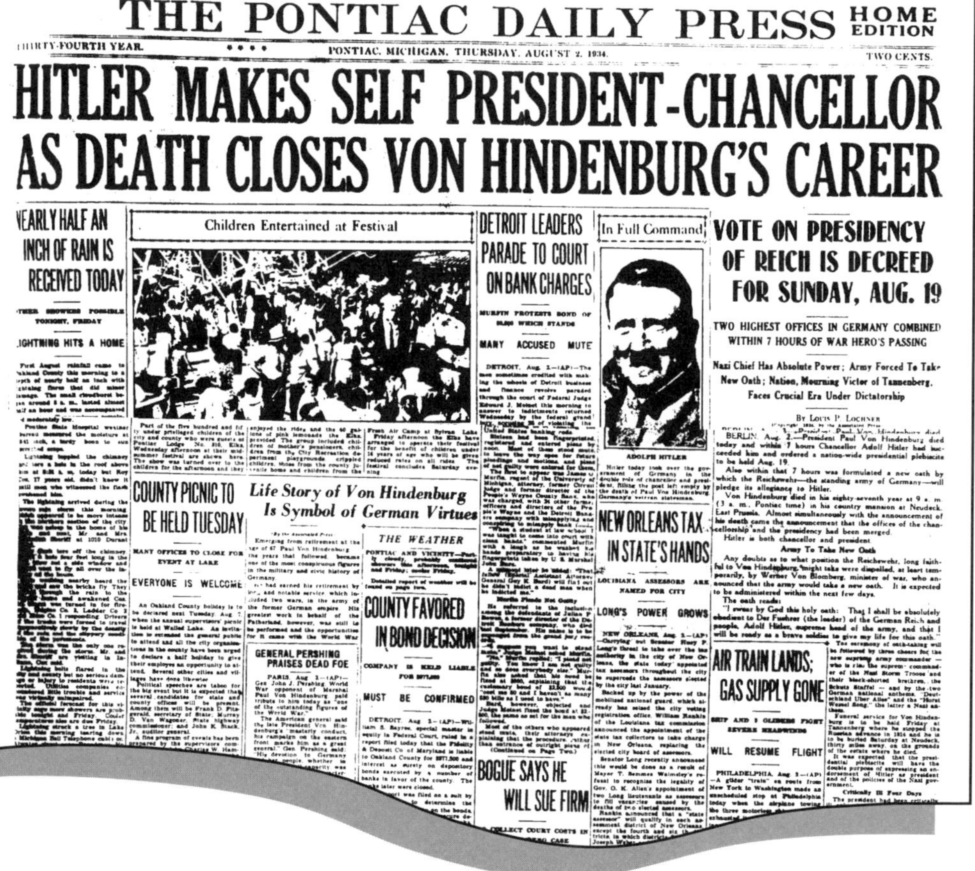

THE PONTIAC DAILY PRESS

HOME EDITION

THIRTY-FOURTH YEAR. PONTIAC, MICHIGAN, THURSDAY, AUGUST 2, 1934. TWO CENTS.

HITLER MAKES SELF PRESIDENT-CHANCELLOR AS DEATH CLOSES VON HINDENBURG'S CAREER

NEARLY HALF AN INCH OF RAIN IS RECEIVED TODAY

LIGHTNING HITS A HOME

Children Entertained at Festival

COUNTY PICNIC TO BE HELD TUESDAY

EVERYONE IS WELCOME

Life Story of Von Hindenburg Is Symbol of German Virtues

GENERAL PERSHING PRAISES DEAD FOE

THE WEATHER

COUNTY FAVORED IN BOND DECISION

MUST BE CONFIRMED

DETROIT LEADERS PARADE TO COURT ON BANK CHARGES

MURFIN PROTESTS BOND OF $1,500 WHICH STANDS

MANY ACCUSED MUTE

DETROIT, Aug. 2—(AP)—The men sometimes credited with making the wheels of Detroit business and finance revolve paraded through the court of Federal Judge Edward J. Moinet this morning to answer to indictments returned Wednesday by the federal grand jury, accusing 26 of violating the United States banking code.

Sixteen had been fingerprinted, registered and entered pleas by noon. Most of them stood mute, to leave the way open for future pleadings and motions, and pleas of not guilty were entered for them.

The first to appear was James O. Murfin, regent of the University of Michigan, attorney, former Circuit Judge and former director of the People's Wayne County Bank, who was charged, with 24 other former officers and directors of the People's Wayne and the Detroit Bankers company with misapplying and conspiring to misapply bank funds.

"When a student at law school I was taught to come into court with clean hands," commented Murfin with a laugh as he washed his hands preparatory to having his fingerprints taken by U. S. Marshal John Baer.

A moment later he added: "That fellow (Special Assistant Attorney General Guy K. Bard) will find out he didn't indict a dead man when he indicted me."

Murfin Pleads Not Guilty

BOGUE SAYS HE WILL SUE FIRM

In Full Command

ADOLPH HITLER

Hitler today took over the government of Germany in the double role of chancellor and president, filling the post left empty by the death of Paul Von Hindenburg, Germany's veteran statesman.

NEW ORLEANS TAX IN STATE'S HANDS

LOUISIANA ASSESSORS ARE NAMED FOR CITY

LONG'S POWER GROWS

VOTE ON PRESIDENCY OF REICH IS DECREED FOR SUNDAY, AUG. 19

TWO HIGHEST OFFICES IN GERMANY COMBINED WITHIN 7 HOURS OF WAR HERO'S PASSING

Nazi Chief Has Absolute Power; Army Forced To Take New Oath; Nation, Mourning Victor of Tannenberg, Faces Crucial Era Under Dictatorship

By Louis P. Lochner

(Copyright, 1934, by the Associated Press)

BERLIN, Aug. 2.—President Paul Von Hindenburg died today and within 7 hours Chancellor Adolf Hitler had succeeded him and ordered a nation-wide presidential plebiscite to be held Aug. 19.

Also within that 7 hours was formulated a new oath by which the Reichswehr—the standing army of Germany—will pledge its allegiance to Hitler.

Von Hindenburg died in his eighty-seventh year at 9 a. m. (3 a. m., Pontiac time) in his country mansion at Neudeck, East Prussia. Almost simultaneously with the announcement of his death came the announcement that the offices of the chancellorship and the presidency had been merged.

Hitler is both chancellor and president.

Army To Take New Oath

Any doubts as to what position the Reichswehr, long faithful to Von Hindenburg, might take were dispelled, at least temporarily, by Werner Von Blomberg, minister of war, who announced that the army would take a new oath. It is expected to be administered within the next few days.

The oath reads:

"I swear by God this holy oath: That I shall be absolutely obedient to Der Fuehrer (the leader) of the German Reich and people, Adolf Hitler, supreme head of the army, and that I will be ready as a brave soldier to give my life for this oath."

The ceremony of oath-taking will be followed by three cheers for the new supreme army commander—

AIR TRAIN LANDS; GAS SUPPLY GONE

WILL RESUME FLIGHT

THE PONTIAC DAILY PRESS (Now *The Oakland Press)* August 2, 1934

Part 1

The Tension and Traumas of the Times (1939)

The first decades of the 20th century saw hundreds of thousands of eager immigrants flock to America in search of better lives than they experienced in their native lands. For a few years, they enjoyed extraordinary opportunities to better themselves and their families.

Then America faced the challenge of The Great Depression from the late 1920s through the middle of the next decade. The economies of many nations went out of control into a prolonged decline. Businesses failed daily and personal hardships became commonplace as jobs disappeared and millions of ordinary citizens, their dreams and hopes shattered, ran out of money to buy even the basic essentials.

President Roosevelt shut down all banks by declaring a bank holiday to reorganize the fundamental economic system and provide some measure of confidence to American citizens that a) the nation was solvent and b) there were better days ahead. In the mid-1930's his broad programs began to take hold and the recovery began. For some, it was agonizingly too late, and there were disastrous results.

But as the economic picture brightened, another ominous threat emerged on the horizon. The Nazi party in Germany, inspired and led by Adolf Hitler, was becoming a power to reckon with, and Europeans were beginning to look over their shoulders as they felt the thunderclouds of war being unleashed by Adolf Hitler throughout the continent.

On September 4, 1939, German forces invaded Poland in a surprise attack. Then, in solidarity with Poland, Great Britain and France declared war on Germany.

The Norwegian government declared a neutral position when war broke out and prepared their military forces to protect the national borders and preserve their neutrality; however, they were unprepared for an invasion.

In mid-December of 1939, the importance of Norway in their plans for naval operations was a subject of considerable discussion by both German and Allied strategists.

The Germans' strategy called for total occupation of Denmark and Norway, tied to the operation of bases for ships and submarines needed for the war at sea. When naval action near the Norwegian seacoast disrupted trans-Atlantic travel and commercial shipping, the effects were felt not only in Norway but in many other countries as well.

Still nursing the economic recovery after the Depression, America turned the corner on the new decade by reluctantly preparing for war. Few government officials or ordinary citizens of the U.S. or European countries would have predicted that Hitler's insatiable hunger for power would drive the world into war for five tragic years. But they soon learned that reality was worse than all predictions and that international events could have a dramatic impact on personal and family plans.

THE HOFF AND OLSEN FAMILIES

OLSENS	BORN	DIED
Johan Didrik Olsen	1873	1945
Ingeborg Marie Nagell Olsen	1873	1937
Ingrid Johanne Olsen Njøsen	1897	1979
Johan Nagell Olsen	1898	1961
Dagmar Fredrikke Olsen	1900	1923
Olga Marie Olsen	1901	1903
Sigurd Martin Olsen	1903	1997
Olga Marie Olsen Hoff	1905	1996

HOFFS		
Mathias Anders Hoff	1873	1945
Andrea Bendiksen Hoff	1873	1953
Anna Hoff Jacobsen	1895	1975
Bernhard Karolius Hoff	1897	1954
Margit Hoff Andersen	1898	1983
Kristine Hoff Birkeland	1900	1970
Carl Hoff	1903	1994
Mathilde Hoff Madsen	1905	1995
Astrid Hoff	1907	1922
Magnus Hoff	1910	1983
Aagot Hoff	1912	1925
Borghilde Hoff	1914	1990
Einar Hoff	1916	—

1
OUR FAMILY'S ROOTS

Dad couldn't think of a better way to celebrate his eighty-fifth birthday than to be surrounded by the people he loved most. Olga, his wife of almost 60 years, was at his side as usual. Karen and I, his daughters, were close at hand helping to serve, organize, and cheerlead the birthday greetings. Enjoying the celebration were sons-in-law, grandchildren, great grandchildren, and other members of the Hoff family who had gathered that day—February 27, 1988—to help Dad blow out the 85 candles.

Despite his advanced years, Dad was in rare form, joking and telling his favorite stories from the past. When he paused to catch his breath, Mom would add her own comments and lead him to yet another story about his experiences as a "greenhorn immigrant," as he called himself. Dad's sense of humor, always one of the best things about him, kept everyone smiling during that enjoyable afternoon.

When we planned this special birthday party, Karen and I decided to videotape the event so that present and future generations of Hoffs could see for themselves the unique qualities of Carl and Olga, our parents, and catch a glimpse of many other family members as well.

After they became aware of the taping, Mom and Dad were excited about the idea and started to think about different stories they wanted to share with everyone. Dad also wanted to make sure he looked his best on the video and, as he had done so often throughout their married years, he turned to Mom to pick out the best shirt and sweater to wear to the party. And when she made her recommendation, he didn't quibble about it, because he knew her taste in clothes was better than his.

She wore her best dress and, as always, her naturally wavy hair looked like she had just spent the previous day at the beauty shop.

Together, they were a picture of happiness and contentment.

We made sure that all of the family's favorite foods were available for snacking. The buffet included many Norwegian favorites like lefser, krumkaker, smørbrød (open-face sandwiches), almond tarts, waffles, and American cupcakes. Oh, don't let me forget bløtkake (cream cake), Dad's favorite dessert.

But the best part of the special day was the presence of so many members of the family, representing four generations. I remember how we all stopped and said "Oh, Yeah!" when someone mentioned that Mom and Dad were responsible for most of the houseful of people who had come to the party. And Karen pointed out that through the years of their long marriage, Mom had waited hand and foot on Dad. Dad just smiled when she made that comment, but said nothing.

In a split second, Clarence (my husband) and Jim (Karen's husband) looked at us and said, in unison: "Hey! Why aren't you more like your Mom? We don't get that kind of treatment!"

Although we had done this routine dozens of times before, we all laughed at their outburst. Dad looked at Clarence and Jim, shrugged his shoulders, and glanced over at Mom, with a loving smirk on his face.

Our parents were a wonderful couple, and we all felt so proud of them. We were also grateful that they had been with us for so long and that, even in their mid-eighties, their minds were sharp and their health had held up reasonably well.

Both Karen and I counted our blessings many times over. When we considered many of the events and experiences of the past, particularly the period of the wartime years, both of us knew the family was extremely lucky that we were able to enjoy a long-term relationship with Mom and Dad, who came here to America in the '20s with no money, no jobs, and no knowledge of the language, the customs, or the culture.

But I'm getting ahead of myself.

To fully appreciate why we have always considered our family to be so special, you have to know something about a few of the people who originally established our roots back in the western part of Norway around Bergen.

Dad used to say that we had more than our share of characters in the Hoff family, and that there must be some other family somewhere that was short-changed. Our Bestefar,* Mathias Hoff, was a good example of the interesting personalities that have kept our family relationships lively.

Bestefar was a large man, but the characteristic I remember most about him was that he was also kind and gentle, and never intimidating. He was not a talkative man; but when he said something, we always paid attention to his comments. We remember that he was loving and compassionate, and he made sure his family was well cared-for. In a good mood, he was a jolly fellow and often his handlebar mustache would sway from side to side when he laughed. When we were kids, we used to stare at him for long periods while his entire body would quiver and shake in spells of hearty laughter. Later, we would all join in the giggling and chuckling. It was quite a

* In Norway, the term for grandfather is "Bestefar"; grandmother is "Bestemor"; father is "Far"; mother is "Mor"; uncle is "Onkel"; and aunt is "Tante."

sight...and sound. Although a lot of years have gone by, I can still remember the echoes of wonderful laughter we all shared.

Bestefar kept his muscles toned by cutting wood each week on a lot across the street from his cabin in Rådalen in Fana on property owned by Christian Rå. Christian and Bestefar were good friends for many years and always enjoyed each other's company. After each sweat-spritzing session of wood-cutting, Bestefar would rest on a chair that he had carved with an axe out of a tree stump, and he and Christian would swig down a beer. At his side was his watchful companion, a reddish brown and white mongrel dog given to him by Dad's youngest brother, Onkel Einar.

A trash collector by trade, Bestefar traveled all over town each day making his rounds and stacking the trash on his buggy, which was pulled by an old horse. Bestefar was very well liked by his customers and they looked forward to his regular visits. Sometimes, when they left empty bottles in the trash, he would save them and turn them in for whatever coins he could get. With this money, he could buy a few bottles of beer to be enjoyed without Bestemor knowing about his beer drinking. Extra bottles of the precious brew were stashed carefully and secretly in the woodpile.

I remember that everyone liked our Bestemor, Andrea Hoff. She was an attractive, tall, and slender woman. In the time we knew her, she always showered her family with a never-ending supply of love and caring, and was the type of woman who always seemed to see sunshine behind the clouds. She encouraged us to smile frequently and her positive outlook rubbed off on all her children, especially our Dad, who was the fifth born child of Mathias and Andrea. There were eleven active, noisy, healthy children in the Hoff family.

One of Bestemor Hoff's unique characteristics was the way she walked with a stiff leg, caused by water on the knee, a condition she suffered during her last pregnancy.

When Dad was a young man growing up in Norway, his family lived in a small two-room flat that housed his parents, all ten of his siblings and himself. When money was tight, Bestefar jokingly threatened to rent out one of the two overcrowded rooms they had and confine all of them to one room.

As tight as their living quarters were, on Sundays the entire Hoff family was expected to be at the dinner table at the same time. Since there weren't enough chairs for everyone to sit down at once, planks were placed between chairs to extend the seating area. As the children finished eating, one by one they would slip down under the table, crawl out the other side and leave the room quietly and with a full stomach.

Dad remembered what it was like to have to scrape to meet the family's financial needs. With eleven kids to support, the Hoff family was constantly short of funds. Consequently, Dad and his brothers and sisters were sent out at an early age to work so the family could exist without asking for government assistance.

His first job was at a sardine factory where his sister worked as well. His job was to slide sardines onto a string, place them in a frame, and take them to the smoke house. The money he earned was turned over to his parents.

Even as a youngster, he had ambitions to exceed the expectations of his family, to prowl the unknown frontier, and to make his mark on the world. And he decided the best place to fulfill his ambitions would be in America.

2
THE DREAMS OF AN ADVENTUROUS MAN

After the conclusion of World War I in 1918, Dad's desire to move to America grew stronger every day. He had read about the United States in newspapers and magazines and was magnetized by the prospect of living in such a strong, big, and free country, so he sent in his application for a visa to the U.S. When Dad informed Bestefar about his intentions to go there, Bestefar told him he thought he was crazy and that the savage Indians in America would scalp him.

The immigration process began when Bestemor wrote to her brother Martin in America and mentioned Dad's growing desire to come to the United States. Though his savings were meager, Martin responded to Bestemor's letter by enclosing a ticket for passage to America with his return letter. Dad would never forget his Onkel's benevolence in creating the opportunity to explore the vast unknown, make a better life for himself and learn as much as he could about the land across the sea.

On August 11,1923, at the age of 20, Dad sailed aboard a crowded ship (he described conditions as "standing room only") to New York, arriving at Ellis Island on August 23. There he and the other immigrants from three or four other ships that had just docked were herded like cattle through the process that was required before they could be admitted to America or, in some cases, returned to their homeland. Medical specialists and doctors were assigned to stations that focused on specific aspects of the physical exam they all had to pass. The confused and anxious immigrants queued up in long lines and awaited their turns to be examined by each specialist; then they waited once again while the medics went through the motions in the next stage of the process.

The challenge of a new language was a problem for immigrants, and Dad did his best to understand what the people in authority were saying so that he would know what to do. At one point in the process, he was given a number "4" tag to wear on his shirt. When he saw the same number on a ferry boat, he concluded that he belonged there, so he climbed aboard and was halfway to Manhattan before someone discovered the mistake. He was returned to Ellis Island and eventually was transported aboard the correct ship to the dock.

When he set foot on Manhattan Island, Dad was thrilled to be able to reach down and touch American soil for the first time. He walked from the dock to the train station at Grand Central, where he boarded the train to Chicago and then on to Duluth. Because he was not blessed with an overabundance of cash, he lived for several days on cans of sardines and packages of crackers he had picked up for $1.00 each on Ellis Island before getting on the ferry boat.

Dad, who was quite a storyteller, remembered the first and last time he ever threw food refuse into the street in New York:

Bananas were not plentiful in Norway because of the high cost of shipping them in. So Norwegians knew about bananas primarily from seeing them in pictures in magazines. After arriving for the first time in New York, I saw bananas hanging everywhere in the markets near the ship dock.

It looked like a jungle in the city. I went inside one of the markets and saw a sign that read "Bananas," so I pitched a 50 cent piece on the counter and pointed to the bananas hanging in stalks on hooks behind the counter. Until the fruit peddler handed me a complete stalk that strained my muscle power, I didn't realize that 50 cents in those days bought a sizable number of ripening bananas. I walked outside and started eating them from the stalk. The challenge then was, what to do with the peels? I noticed some garbage in the curb on the street, so I began to toss the peels into the gutters.

In a short time, a policeman approached me and said something like "Hey! What are you doing? Would you do that in your own home? Pick up the peels!"

Of course, I couldn't understand a word the officer said. But from his motions and the tone of his voice, I surmised that he wanted me to pick up the peels I had left behind. I wound up going back and retracing my steps three or four blocks to retrieve every one of the peels I had discarded along the way.

That was the first and last time I have ever thrown food refuse into the street.

Another favorite "new arrival" story Dad loved to tell also involved food. This time, it was pea soup.

When I first arrived in America, my English language was limited to a few key words that got me through the day. For example, when I went to a restaurant, I knew how to order pea soup. That's all.

After several weeks of a pea soup diet, I got tired of pea soup and wanted something else to eat. So I listened for the order placed with the waiter by the people at the next table.

"Ham sandwich" is what they said, so I said the same words when the waiter asked me for my order.

But then he continued to stand next to my table and I started to think I may have done something wrong. Then he spoke.

"Sir, would you like your ham sandwich on white or rye?"

Flustered and unprepared for that question, I could only respond with words that I knew: PEA SOUP!

And so, before I knew it, I was soon dipping my spoon in yet another bowl of the dreaded pea soup.

Later, on the train to Minnesota, the conductor asked around to see if any of the other passengers could speak Norwegian. One man came forward, and the conductor brought him to meet Dad. Coincidentally, the man had known Dad's parents in Norway and had come to the United States in 1903 with Dad's Onkel Martin. When they arrived in Duluth, the man took Dad home with him and called Onkel Martin to let him know where he could come and pick Dad up.

At the time, Onkel Martin was renting one room in a boarding house. There wasn't room for both him and Dad, so they found new accommodations at a Finnish boarding house. The cost: $3.00 per week for room and $6.00 per week for board. Then, Martin helped him find a job in the lumber yard of a box factory where he was employed, about 20 miles from Duluth. They worked there for about four months, and both men decided to go to Duluth to look for a new job.

They were hired to spike rails for the railroad, a job Dad remembered as the most physically-challenging he ever experienced. After four months, they were once again ready to move on. Dad recalled that the Norwegian-speaking man he met on the train had told him that if he ever needed a job to "look him up." So he contacted the man and he found new jobs for him and Onkel Martin in Duluth that paid 55 cents per hour.

Dad thought he had struck it rich, and soon purchased a 1925

Chevy Touring car for $800, splurging on extras like side curtains and a toolbox.

Meanwhile, back in Norway, his brother Ben was closely following Dad's progress and was aware that he had a job that paid a good salary, so he asked him to send money to enable him to finish his schooling. Dad sent him the money, but Ben used it to travel to Canada, where he worked briefly in the construction business, and eventually joined Dad in Duluth. From there he moved to the Detroit area, where he began to work for the Ford Motor Company.

Dad and Onkel Martin stayed on in Duluth a little while longer, but they didn't like it there and decided to leave their jobs and follow Ben to Michigan where they were hoping to land jobs in the automotive industry just as Ben had. First, they applied for jobs at Ford in Highland Park, but the company told them the workforce was not being expanded at that time.

Having grown up close to the ocean in Norway, Dad missed being near the water, so almost every day when he was in Highland Park he would walk down Woodward Avenue to the riverfront in Detroit, a distance of about 6 miles, just to view the current, check out the success of some fishermen and watch the boats go by.

After being without work for over three weeks, the three of them headed for Pontiac to apply for work at Pontiac Motors on Oakland Avenue. To their surprise, the company hired them immediately and asked them to consider starting that same day. Dad and Onkel Ben begged off because they needed time to find a place to live. He also wanted to be close to his place of employment, so he moved to 75 Lafayette in Pontiac before starting his new job. The layoffs of the Great Depression notwithstanding, his job with Pontiac Motors started in 1925 and lasted a little more than 40 years.

3
A DECADE IN AMERICA

The families of our Mom and Dad lived as neighbors for a long time. Mom was only three years old when her family, the Olsens, moved into the flat next to the Hoff family in Bergen. There was always a lot of social interaction between the two families, and Mom used to assist Dad's mother around the house, helping to set up the nightly beds and making open-faced sandwiches for everyone before bedtime.

Mom and Dad had begun dating during their teenage years and, as one wartime letter makes apparent, had liked each other quite well at that time. During a visit to Norway in 1927, Dad worked up the courage to ask Mom to marry him. However, she felt that as the last of five children in her family she had obligations to her aging mother, so she asked Dad to be patient while she worked out her family situation. That decision must have been extremely difficult for her, because she was obviously in love with him.

Dad returned to America alone, but he knew that Mom was committed to him and that they were, in effect, engaged. About two years later, they were married in Norway on a cold and rainy day, the second of November, 1929. Mom wore a beautiful wedding dress that Dad had bought for her at Hudson's in Detroit.

Their honeymoon was spent at the country house of Dad's parents in Rådalen in the northern region of Fana. To their surprise, Dad's brother Ben, who had also traveled back to Norway for their wedding, had somehow invited himself along on the honeymoon. Dad returned to America after the honeymoon, but Mom was not able to make the trip to New York until January of 1930 because she had to wait for her visa to come through. Dad met her in New York and they took the train back to Michigan..

Throughout his married life, Dad was always concerned about advancing the family's well-being. He was devoted to Mom and we never heard them express harsh words to each other. Having developed a keen sense of curiosity, his active mind carried him into a love affair with history. A serious reader, he would often start and finish a book well before anyone else in the family had even reached the half-way point.

On the other hand, Mom was a more methodical person who planned family activities with meticulous detail. She was a typical Scandinavian woman—tall, attractive, self-assured. She looked after us with great care, always making sure we put the right foot forward, and that we handled ourselves with grace and class. We were usually very shy and reserved, but she helped us develop confidence and good social skills. An accomplished seamstress, she outfitted us fashionably while we were growing up.

As Dad settled into his job with Pontiac Motors, he was able to put away a small amount of money from each paycheck and found after a couple of years that he could afford to buy some property he had been looking at in the suburban town of Auburn Heights. So Mom and Dad made an offer and had it accepted. But when it came time for them to build on the lot, there was no money—and the only way they could afford to fulfill their dreams was to get a loan from Sears, Roebuck and Company. Since they already had paid for the lot, Sears Ok'd their application for the financing of a home kit that included all materials and instructions for the construction of a house.

So with help from friends and neighbors, Dad and Mom painstakingly built, by hand, their first homestead. At last they had their own place to call home, and they enjoyed happy times there during the eight years they owned it.

When I was born on June 5, 1932, I arrived "paid in full." At that time, the cost of delivering a baby was $35.00. So in typical fashion, each month, Mom and Dad paid a dollar or two to the doctor, so the account was paid up when I was delivered by Dr. William Green, who at that time was a young doctor just starting his practice. He stayed in the Pontiac area for many years and brought over 20,000 babies into the world before he retired at the age of 84. Eight of those babies were delivered into our family alone, including Karen who was born in December of 1935.

As the eldest daughter, I accompanied Mom on a trip to Norway in 1935 when I was just three years old. Mom often told me this visit to Norway was very important to her because she wanted her parents to get to know me, their only grandchild. Karen never had the opportunity to meet Mom's mother, since she died on Karen's second birthday in December of 1937.

Since Mom and Dad came to America ten years earlier, they had struggled through the Great Depression and were among many Americans who did their best to cope with the lack of work. Knowing my Dad as well as Karen and I did, we are absolutely convinced that if there had been any work to do, Dad would have gone after it. Instead, he pitched horseshoes with other men who were unemployed, just to pass the time. Being out of work eventually meant that, no matter how hard they tried, they were unable to meet their financial obligations.

He had worked hard at Pontiac Motors to earn and save the

money to buy a lot, then build their home in Auburn Heights, but jobs came and went in those times and Dad's work dried up when car sales declined.

The monthly house payment was only $28.00, but since there was no money coming in, they were not able to pay it. They went to the bank that held the mortgage to see what they could do and the bank allowed them to stay in their home one more year without having to make any payments. The banker realized that no one had any money at that time so the house was not likely to be sold or rented to anyone else; they agreed, therefore, that Mom and Dad would take care of the house as long as they could live there.

Regrettably, I spent three months in the hospital around this same time with scarlet fever and languished with the illness for almost a full year. A lifelong hearing deficiency resulted from my bout with the disease.

With all of our options depleted, the time came for us to move out of our home. We had no alternative but to move in with Dad's sister, Margit Andersen, and her family, who lived just a couple of blocks away from our homestead. (Margit had come to America later in 1923, the same year as Dad's arrival.) In the meantime, we prayed that our situation might change.

After some serious discussions, Mom and Dad finally agreed that it might be best for them to move to Norway and take advantage of the family support system in their homeland. Mom was against the idea that she would take us first, and that Dad would follow in a few months. He felt positive about the need for us to get an early start in adapting to our new homeland. After all, we had to learn the language, become familiar with local customs, and adjust to Norwegian foods and cooking.

He figured he wasn't needed for all of that, and that Mom was quite capable of looking after us during this transition. Meanwhile, he could continue his job at Pontiac Motors and build up our nest egg of savings so we never would have to rely on anyone else to help us meet our financial obligations.

After the difficult times of the Depression years, he felt that a steady job in hand was worth the sacrifice of living apart temporarily. And so, the long-awaited day was finally here. It was August 20, 1939, and Mom, Karen, and I along with Mom's sister Ingrid Olsen were in New York getting ready to board the M.S. *Oslofjord* for our journey to Norway. We'd said good-bye to Dad in Michigan, since there wasn't enough money for him to come to New York to see us off. In addition, he didn't want to take time off from his job and lose more money.

With the ship's crew making final preparations to depart, we could see energetic young porters wheeling bag after bag up the ramp and into the passengers' staterooms. Noise seemed to come from everywhere; from the taxies down below, tooting their horns to clear their path, to the loud voices of the people at the rail as they shouted good-byes to their loved ones on the dock.

Though I was a big girl of seven, my little hand was wrapped tightly in Mom's and I tried to wave the other hand, but that one got tired and I had to stop waving altogether. I just grinned at anyone who looked at me. Although the ship had not departed, I was already beginning to miss my friends in Auburn Heights, and I wondered whether I would make new friends after I settled in Bergen, Norway, our destination.

Eventually, all the good-byes were shouted, and the ship started to move. We felt unsteady for the first time. I wondered whether we were going to have that shaky feeling in our legs for the entire trip, and Mom reassured me that I would get used to the ship's movement, as we had on our earlier journey.

Mom had looked forward to this sailing for a very long time. Living in America had been wonderful in many ways, but she missed Norway, her family, her friends, and the memories she left behind when she moved to America with Dad ten years earlier. She was determined to prepare for a new life back in Norway, where we would have a safety net of family support to help deal with challenges that might threaten our progress in the future.

She had spent many hours planning the trip, and she was anxious to get back to her homeland. However, she couldn't imagine being apart from Dad for any length of time, but she was certain that being halfway around the world from him would cause her great anxiety.

Even so, to unite her daughters with the "old country" family would be the fulfillment of a dream for her, an opportunity to link together the two arms of the Hoff and Olsen families for the first time since they moved from Norway in 1929.

She looked forward to showing off her girls to everyone they had known before leaving Norway ten years earlier.

Mom was sure that despite the uncertainty of the international situation, everything would turn out all right.

As far as I was concerned, the journey to Bergen was just a vacation trip. I believed that we would return to Auburn Heights and resume our friendships and other activities there. But I had no way of knowing that, for the next six years, Norway—not Auburn Heights—was to be our home.

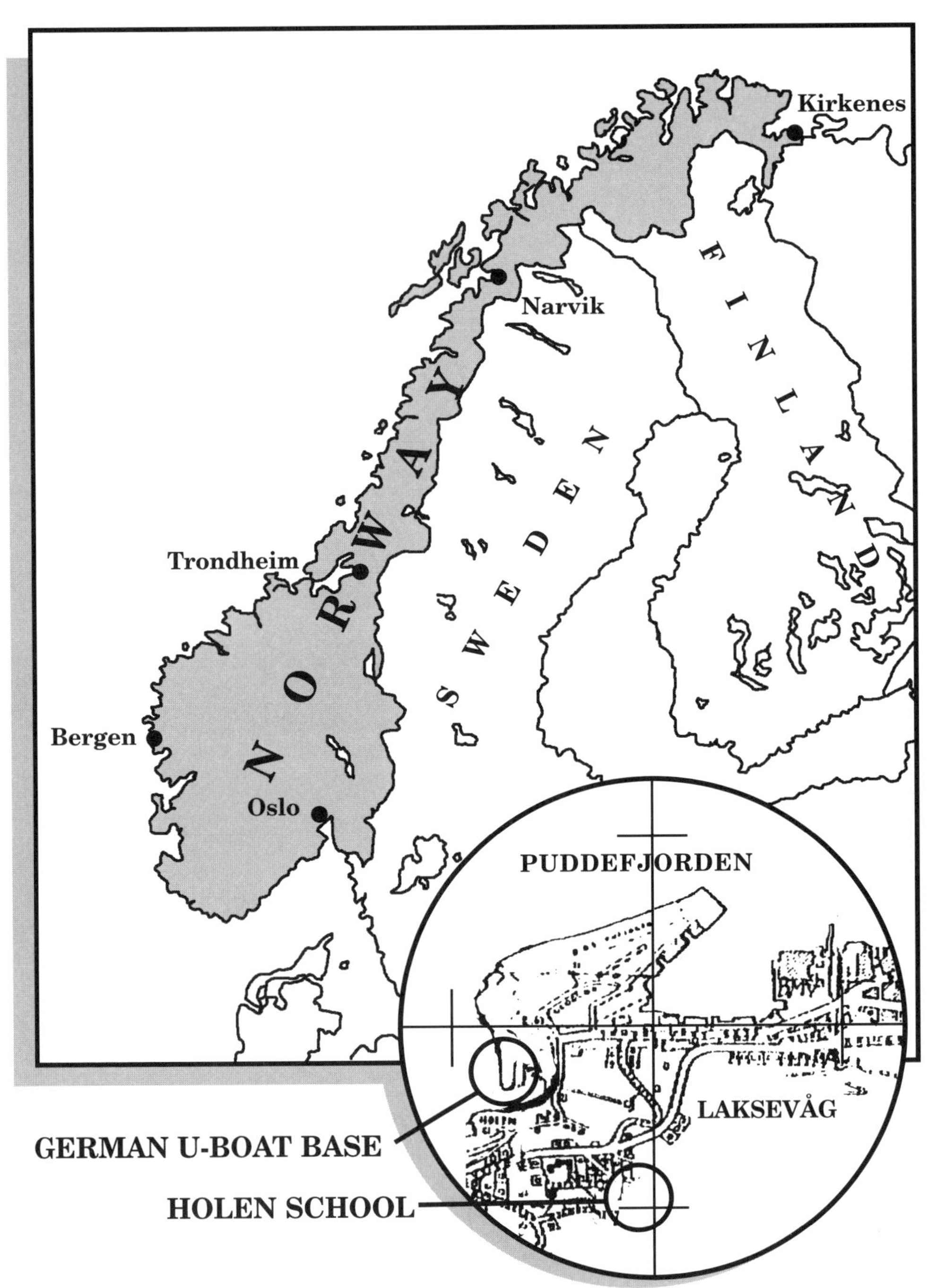
Kirkenes
Narvik
FINLAND
SWEDEN
NORWAY
Trondheim
Bergen
Oslo
PUDDEFJORDEN
LAKSEVÅG
GERMAN U-BOAT BASE
HOLEN SCHOOL

4
BACK ON NORWEGIAN SOIL, MINUS ONE

Though our trip across the Atlantic Ocean started with calm seas and beautiful weather, about three days out of New York we were attacked by a storm that whipped across the bow of our ship and gave us a ride that only a hardy seaman could appreciate. Seasickness was the order for the day and we wound up spending much of our time in bed.

We couldn't eat, because no food would stay down. Three long days after the storm arrived, it departed and serene waters returned. The remainder of our trip was pleasant, but because of the storm the captain radioed ahead that our arrival would be a day later than planned. There were no cheers from the passengers when that announcement was made.

At 5:00 p.m. on August 30, 1939, the *Oslofjord* motored slowly through the harbor of Bergen and positioned itself at the dock. Sailors ran to attach lines around cleats in the cement dock. All the passengers were on deck to wave at the people lining the pier and calling out their enthusiastic greetings. To us, their shouted comments were gibberish. To Mom, their Norwegian words raised goosebumps. She was home.

As we made our way down the ramp, we were greeted by both Dad's and Mom's relatives. Though we were happily overwhelmed by the warm welcome extended by our Norwegian family, we were even more pleased to be on solid ground once again. Our sea legs were shaky and we felt far removed from the world we had known back in

America. And we all missed Dad.

Tante Ingrid, who had traveled with us on the ship, helped Mom find an apartment in Laksevåg, a small community near Bergen. Meanwhile, we stayed with Mom's brother, Sigurd, and his wife, Ingeborg, until our apartment was ready. The plan was for Mom, Karen, and me to share the new apartment with Ingrid and Bestefar Johan Didrik Olsen (Mom and Ingrid's dad). Bestefar had been living with his son, Johan Nagell Olsen, but had not been happy there because he didn't feel welcome.

Tante Ingrid found work quickly because of her hat designing experience in Chicago. She was hired as soon as she applied for a job at Sundt's, Bergen's finest department store.

Mom and Tante Ingrid began to assemble a collection of furniture for the apartment. Mom bought beds for us that would be usable as we grew, but since Tante Ingrid was the only employed person in the family, she purchased most of the other furniture we needed. The pieces she bought were unfinished, so she arranged to have them painted red with blue trim.

At the same time, Mom and Tante Ingrid bought coal for the impending fall and winter weather. It was a big help for Mom when Bestefar offered to pay most of the rent from his pension check. Mom's contribution was to buy food, cook, clean, and care for her family.

With war clouds drifting from some of the European capitals south of Norway, both Mom and Dad became concerned about Dad's planned voyage back to his homeland. Great Britain had planted mines in the North Sea that made it unsafe to travel, and indeed, shortly after our arrival in Bergen, the shipping routes and schedule of the Norwegian/American Line were adjusted to ensure the safety of crews and passengers. The early letters between Mom and Dad were dependent upon the schedule of these ships, and though they were able to correspond, more and more delays were being encountered.

We moved into our new apartment on October 17 and all of us were happy to have a place of our own. I started Holen School a week later and because I came from America, I received celebrity treatment from the other children.

I liked school, especially writing and math, and had little difficulty making friends. One day I came home and sang a new song I had learned in Norwegian. My performance made Mom laugh, for I can't carry a tune and my rendition was less than perfect, but she appreciated my effort and praised me enthusiastically for trying to impress her.

Soon after moving into the apartment, I began spending much of my free time with Olga Hansen (Mossa), a girl in our neighborhood. We became best friends and to this day we still keep in touch with each other.

Karen was full of mischief at that time and seemed to grow up very quickly from day to day. She stayed close to Mom most of her waking hours and, as Mom put it, "Karen is less of a crybaby since moving to Norway."

We had a good time visiting all of our aunts and uncles and grandparents. Bestefar Olsen took us to the park every day to play. Dad's youngest sister, Tante Borghild, was not working, so she went everywhere with us as well.

We visited with Dad's parents often. Bestefar liked the shirt we had brought him while Bestemor expressed appreciation for the material Mom had brought to make a dress for her.

The move to Norway had gone smoothly so far, but now Mom was feeling somewhat depressed because she hadn't received a letter from Dad for several weeks. She checked repeatedly with the Norwegian/American Line offices in Bergen to find out when the next ship was due in and was informed that the next scheduled arrival was on October 20. She was hoping with all her heart that it would carry letters from Dad.

The ship did come in as she had been told and Mom received ten letters from America along with packages, magazines, and newspaper clippings. She felt like a new person with all this mail, though some of the letters were dated more than a month earlier.

Her elation soon faded. As she read Dad's letters, Mom began to worry about how sad he was at being separated from his family. She immediately wrote to him and told him to come to Norway as soon as possible and not to worry about saving so much money.

Dad also fretted in his letters about the progress of the war in Europe. Mom tried to ease his mind by telling him that we were all fine and that the problems between Finland and Russia would be settled in a short time, and settled peaceably. Mom then wrote Dad that she felt everything would be all right, but that our patience would be tested.

Indeed it was. Mom was very lonely, and we could hear her crying herself to sleep many nights. One evening, Karen heard her crying and asked if she had a stomach ache. Mom thought to herself, "Oh, if it were only that simple."

Even at this early stage of their separation, Mom was beginning to feel that her return to Norway without Dad was a mistake.

She would get no argument from him on that conclusion. Our dad had both high hopes and great expectations when he left Norway in

1923. After all, America had become known as the land of opportunity. But many of his fantasies had faded and sixteen years after he had started chasing the great American dream, he wasn't sure he was going to realize his lofty ambitions. On the plus side, he was married to Mom and the love they shared was extraordinarily special. And, of course, there were Karen and me. Dad thoroughly enjoyed having two daughters.

But after we left for Norway, he felt frustrated that his life was so dominated by events and situations he couldn't control. Lonely and relegated to an uncomfortable living environment with his sister and her husband, since he couldn't afford a separate apartment, he began to write letters every day to Mom, Karen, and me. Together with his job at Pontiac Motors, the daily letter-writing routine helped him stay sane during these trying times.

What follows are various portions of our Mom's letters to Dad as we left America and they show her happiness as well as her sadness and struggles to make a new home for us in those first months before the Germans invaded Norway. Mom's pet name for Dad was "Calle" or "Calleman" and that's the name she used in addressing her letters.

August 24, 1939 (En route to Norway on board the Oslofjord*)*

My Dear Calleman,

How are you doing? We are all fine and the weather is beautiful. The food is good and we all have healthy appetites. Karen and Dossi each got a dollar from Onkel Ben for their trip and we received a basket of fruit while visiting at Agnes' house.

August 28, 1939

Landing cards were handed out today. There are only 235 passengers on board, including many elderly couples who have been visiting their children in America. I promise to write the day after we land. Many thousands of greetings from the three of us.

Olga, Dossi, and Karen

September 1, 1939

Hello, Calleman,

How are you, my darling? I am already anxiously awaiting a letter from you. Well, I better begin where I left off in my last letter. We really had it nice the last two days on the ship. The Captain's dinner was delicious and afterwards we had some entertainment that was very good. There was music, song and jokes. Also there were six couples, all dressed in Norwegian National costumes, and they danced many of the old folk dances. Everyone liked them very much and clapped their hands till they were sore.

At 1:30 that evening we could see light in the distance. The weather was still and clear. The next day we arrived in Bergen in beautiful sunshine. The approach to Bergen was wonderful. Dossi and Karen were so surprised and happy to see land. At 3:30 p.m. we docked in Bergen. Not everyone could come and meet us at the dock that time of day, but just the same there were many there to greet us.

Your Mom looks real good, Calle, and your Dad is the same, but heavier than I remember. Everyone was very enthusiastic over the children. They thought Dossi was very pretty It is true and she is so sweet. Everyone thought that Karen looked like you.

Love from all of us.

Olga.

P.S. Is it true the war has started in Europe?

September 6, 1939

My Dear Calleman,

We are all fine, but it is terrible that the war has started in Europe. Don't worry about us; I am sure we will be okay The girls are having a good time. They go to Nygårds Park every morning with their Bestefar. Dossi and Karen have slowly begun to talk a little Norwegian, but I don't want to start Dossi in school until we have an apartment and know where we are going to live. I look for the postman every morning, hoping for a letter from you. I hope all is well with you, Calle, and don't worry about us.

Greetings from the heart from all three of us.

September 26, 1939

A thousand thanks for all your letters and cards and the pictures. Dossi took your picture out to show all her friends and said, "This is my daddy." She is doing well with her Norwegian and has lots of friends. I am glad the girls are doing well. I like it here, also. Calle, if only you were here.

We have found an apartment in Laksevåg, Calleman. It is very hard to find an apartment and we have to take what we can get. There are three rooms, a bath, and a kitchen with a wonderful view of the harbor. After October 17 our address will be Nygjerdet 14,

Laksevåg. I wonder how things will go with this war? What do you think, Calle, and what are they saying in America? Please take care.

I love you, Daddy.

Love from all of us.

<u>*September 27, 1939*</u>

My Dear Man,

I got two more letters today and the check. I can't tell you how I feel right now for I will start to cry. Don't worry about us, Calle, for we are fine. I will be glad when we are in our own apartment. I don't want you to feel bad about us being apart for a while. I have to believe we will be together soon. It will be hard for a while, but just think about how wonderful it will be when we are back together.

Please take care of yourself for me and the girls.

<u>*October 18, 1939*</u>

My Darling,

It has been a long time since I've had a letter. I know it is not your fault now that the war is going on. I don't think we will get our mail on a regular basis anymore. God knows I miss you and a letter would do wonders for me. Calle, you must come home to me as soon as possible. There will always be a way for us to make it. I feel tonight that you are so far away from me. I will feel better when I get a letter. We moved yesterday and now it is two o'clock in the morning so I guess I had better go to bed. Good night, darling. The girls are sleeping so sweetly. I am glad they don't have to suffer as we do.

<u>*October 19, 1939*</u>

I cried myself to sleep last night. I went to bed about two o'clock but did not go to sleep for a long time. I woke up this morning with a big headache so I took two aspirins so I could get myself together. I am feeling much better tonight. I went to Laksevåg to get some bread and at the same time I called the steamship office to see what time the Bergensfjord *would be coming in. They told me eleven o'clock tonight. I was so happy and now have new hope of getting a letter tomorrow. It is now ten o'clock so I will sit over in the window and watch for the ship to come in. We have a wonderful view from here. I am so restless and anxious just thinking about a letter from you. I am sure I will sleep better tonight once I see that ship come in.*

<u>*October 20, 1939*</u>

I feel like a new woman today. I received lots of mail on Friday. I was so disappointed because no mail had arrived here for me, but when I called Ingeborg she said the mail had still come to the old address. She said there was so much mail and so many packages that the postman thought he was going to need a wagon. You can't believe how happy that made me. The letters were over a month old, Calle, but now the sadness is over for I have so much to read. It is amazing what your letters do for my spirit. We are all fine and healthy. Well, I had better stop for now so I can get this letter on the ship tomorrow.

Love, Olga, Dossi, and Karen

November 5, 1939

Hello Darling,

How are you? I long after you every minute and everywhere I go I think about you. How long do you think we can go on like this, Calleman? Here we are in different parts of the world missing and dreaming about each other. It is not easy but we must do the best we can. The girls are fine and doing well. If only you were here we could take the girls for a walk on this beautiful day. Dossi likes school a lot and you won't believe what a fast learner she is. I am used to them talking Norwegian now but it makes me laugh when I hear Karen mix her English and Norwegian. She has two small braids now and looks real cute. Well, Calle, the last letter I had from you was eighteen pages on both sides and I loved it. Please take care of yourself and don't worry about us. Don't believe everything you read in the paper. We do get enough to eat.

Good night, darling.

November 15, 1939

Hello Calleman,

On Friday it will be three weeks since your last letter, and at that time you were so depressed. I am hoping to hear that you are better by now. I know how you feel, Calle, for I feel the same sometimes. It is hard being apart from each other. I know it won't be easy to get a job over here, but maybe you will get lucky. Just don't think you have to have several thousand dollars saved before you come, for we need you, Calle. Dossi and I sat here in the window last night talking about you. She started to cry and said she wished you had come with us. "Poor Daddy," she said and then I started to cry. Then I thought I'd better pull myself together so we started talking about how much fun we will have when you come. She felt better before she went to bed.

I am sure we will find a way to make things work, Calle, so please come as soon as you can. I don't know how I could have left without you. We have been apart three months now but it seems like an eternity. Life is so empty without you. We had both good times and bad times when we were together, but we always did the best we could. Take care of yourself for us.

Dossi is doing fine in school. Yesterday her whole class was weighed and the doctor thought Dossi was a little too thin. He suggested things for her to eat and to give her vitamins. She weighs 22 kilograms and is 125 centimeters tall. Will write more tomorrow.

Good night, darling.

November 22, 1939

Hello Darling,

How are you? It is getting close to Christmas so this might be your Christmas letter. Everything is the same here, Calle, and we are all fine and healthy. Ingrid and I have a lot of work to do and I have many orders to make children's clothes. I am working on a coat now and have to make three dresses. I get six kroner for the coat and three and a half for each of the dresses. I sat up till midnight last night working on the coat for it had to be ready for today.

Today I washed clothes. It is not so bad washing these days as it used to be. I soak the white clothes in soap water and then the next day boil them in the kettle. Then I let them lay in rinse water for a couple of hours. The colored clothes I wash on a wash board.

On Friday it will be four weeks since my last letter from you, Calle. I know it takes time now for all the mail is opened and inspected. I went to town yesterday to get a schedule of when the ships will sail, but they had none for 1940 for everything is so uncertain these days.

I went to the basement and got the clothes and Dossi just came home, so now I will have to start dinner. Tonight I have to sew for I have a lot of sewing waiting to be done. I am sure I will be busy sewing from now till Christmas. I like working at home so I can take care of the girls. They are doing just fine and look real good. Sigurd and Ingeborg are coming here Christmas Eve and the first Christmas day we are going to their house and second Christmas day we are going to your Mom and Dad's for dinner.

Well, Calle, it is now four o'clock and I just finished with the clothes so now I will hurry to town and mail your letter. I will take the girls with me for they like to ride the ferry. I hope you are okay. You won't believe how much I miss you and long for a letter from you. I love you so much, Calle, and it is so painful to be so far apart from you. I feel so helpless sometimes. I will be waiting and hoping for a letter from you next week.

Well, the girls are waiting and say "hello" to their daddy. Dossi will write you for Christmas. She is learning Christmas songs in school now, so she goes around singing "Glade Jul." Well, darling, take care of yourself. I am thinking about you every minute and miss you and long to see your sweet face.

<u>*December 14, 1939*</u>

I just got a long letter from you so now I am happy. I also got four packages from you with magazines and lots of other reading stuff. A large American ship came in yesterday afternoon and I thought to myself that there must be a letter for me on that boat, and there was. It had been mailed November 6 and it had been opened.

I see the American ship is still docked in the harbor, so I will mail this today in case the ship takes off in the middle of the night. Well, darling, everything is fine with us and we are all well. Last Tuesday I took the girls to town to look at all the Christmas lights. Sundt's has a beautiful display. It is six o'clock now and I hear the girls coming in. They look so red in their faces. It must be the cold fresh air. Dossi does not have school till 11:30 tomorrow so they can stay up a little later tonight. You know how much I love you and miss you. I send a letter a week hoping that you will get them sooner or later. I am looking forward to us being together again. If only you were here now I would take care of you. How about breakfast in bed with coffee cream and one of those cinnamon buns you like so well? Don't worry about this war, Calle, for we will be all right. You know how much I love you, darling, for you are so wonderful.

<u>*December 31, 1939*</u>

Well, today is the last day of 1939 and I am glad. It is now 11:30 and the girls are sound asleep. They have been outside playing all day. At night they are so tired they fall asleep in a minute. I am glad to be alone with you tonight, Calle. I want to think about next

New Year's Eve when we will be together. We always stayed at home on New Year's Eve, right Calle? Do you remember when Dossi was little we took her out of her bed at midnight and the three of us just sat together for a while? The church bells are ringing now, so it must be midnight. Thank you for the old year, darling, and I hope the new year will be better for us.

Good night for now, Calleman. I love you.

Thus, on a hopeful note, Mom ends her final letter of 1939 to Dad.

From the Photo Album

Dad's entire family is shown in this 1917 photo. From left in the back row are Carl (our Dad), Kristine, Ben, Anna, and Margit. In the front row are Magnus, Bestemor Andrea holding Einar, Astrid, Mathilde, Aagot (in front) and Bestefar Mathias holding Borghild.

Bestefar Hoff making his daily rounds to pick up trash. The boy in the picture is Stanley Hoff, Onkel Ben's son who was visiting from America in 1935.

Mathias and Andrea Hoff, our grandparents.

Bestemor Ingeborg and Bestefar Johan Olsen, Mom's parents.

Our great grandfather, Anders Ludvikson Hoff, lived to the age of 100 (1838-1938). The boy in the picture is Stanley Hoff.

Mathias Hoff and his father, Anders, with Stanley.

Passport photo of dad in 1923, the year he journeyed to America for the first time.

Dad's early jobs in Duluth, Minnesota, included working on the railroad, where he spiked rails. After a time in Minnesota, he moved on to Michigan, where he began a 40-year career with Pontiac Motors. These photos were taken in 1924.

Onkel Martin, Dad, and Onkel Ben, shown in 1926.

Olga Hoff in Norway (1927)

Left, Mom and Dad in 1927.
Below left, Mom and Dad's engagement picture.
Below, wedding on November 2, 1929.

Mom and Dad in front of the house they built in Auburn Heights in 1931.

Catherine (Dossi) at three.

Karen Marie Hoff shown at 9 months.

Our Mom with Tante Ingrid.

Bestemor Ingeborg and Bestefar Johan with Dossi, in 1935.

Tante Ingrid, Mom, and Dossi in 1935 during Dossi's first trip to Norway.

Karen, Tante Ingrid, and Dossi on board the M.S. Oslofjord in 1939.

A day at the zoo with dad (1937).

Dressed to meet family in Norway.

EXTRA

THE PONTIAC DAILY PRESS

NAZIS INVADE POLAND; CAPITAL CITY BOMBED

WARSAW, Sept. 1.—(UP)—German airplanes bombed the Polish capital at 9 a. m. (3 a. m. Pontiac time) today, it was announced officially, within an hour after German bombardments had been reported in five other cities in Poland.

The foreign office immediately charged Germany with aggression, announcing: "Shortly after 7 a. m. Germans started military action at different points on the frontier. This undoubtedly is German aggression against Poland. Military action developing."

The foreign office did not name the places of action.

It was reported that the German bombing squadrons had not been large.

The government announced that they had bombed among other places, the railway station at Czew,' the town of Rypnic and the town

Hitler's order to his army was issued at 5:30 a. m. (11:30 p. m., EST., Thursday).

"The German army will conduct a fight for honor and the right to the life of the resurrected German people with firm determination," [illegible] said.

[illegible] REJECTED OFFER

FREE CITY RETURNS TO REICH

BERLIN, Sept. 1.—(AP)—The German official news agency, DNB, announced today that Albert Forster, Nazi chief of state in Danzig, had proclaimed the reunion of the free city with the Reich.

Forster notified Adolf Hitler, fuehrer of Germany, of his action, by telegram.

Article one of Forster's decree suspended the constitution of the free city immediately.

(Under the city's League of Nations status its constitution was guaranteed by the league and changes without its consent were declared illegal).

Article 2 of the decree [illegible] legal and administrative power exclusively in the hands of the chief of state, Forster.

Text of Forster Telegram

Forster's telegram to Hitler read: "My fuehrer: I have just signed and then put into effect the following basic law concerning the [illegible] with the German [illegible]

He Arbitrates With Guns

LATE BULLETINS ON WAR

[illegible]

Hitler Denies Force

BERLIN, Sept. 1.—AP—Adolf Hitler, addressing a special session of the Reichstag session today declared that it is a "lie that we do all by force."

Reichstag Summoned

BERLIN, Sept. 1—(AP)—Adolf Hitler summoned the Reichstag to meet at 10 a. m. (4 a. m. Pontiac Time).

From early morning electricians installed loudspeakers in the principal parts of the city. Before the chancellery an unusually large detachment of S. S. men formed a protective cordon.

Members of the Reichstag who had been awaiting the call in the capital since Thursday all wore uniforms. In ministries, [illegible]

THE PONTIAC DAILY PRESS (Now *The Oakland Press)* September 1, 1939

Part 2

The War Years (1940-44)

On April 9, 1940, Hitler's troops took Norway by surprise in a series of attacks throughout the country. The intrusions were met by weak and unsuccessful resistance, for Norwegian troops were poorly organized, underequipped, and unprepared to defend their homeland, and it was quickly overrun.

Before the final capitulation, the only success achieved by the Norwegians was the recapturing of Narvik in the northern region in collaboration with Allied forces. A British naval force reached Narvik and quickly destroyed the German fleet, resulting in Germany's first defeat in three years of war. After the Allies left, however, the Germans retook the city and occupied it for the next five years.

Farther south along the coast, in Trondheim, the harbor was guarded by Norwegian gun batteries that were supposed to destroy any intruders. But when German ships approached, the guns failed to fire, and the enemy troops were able to conveniently disembark at the city docks without interference. As a result, the Germans had control of an excellent harbor capable of accommodating the largest warships and submarines, and providing easy access to the railhead of a rail line that stretched across north central Norway and Sweden.

In Bergen, 300 miles south, the Germans experienced resistance. Here harbor batteries of guns severely damaged several ships coming into their range, but German troops from other vessels were able to land and take control of the city. Although successful in their invasion, the Germans suffered substantial losses of warships when British forces attacked their vessels by air and by sea. German paratroopers secured the airport, preventing the British from landing any large contingents of ground forces.

In Oslo, two large ships were delayed in docking as a result of resistance, but the capital city fell when

Germans took control of the airport in Oslo as well.

When the Germans later deployed their full complement of troops, there were 400,000 occupation forces in Norway, causing shortages of food and supplies until the end of the war.

In 1942, construction began on a German submarine base in Laksevåg, an ideal location for the Germans. For anyone else, however, the selection of the Bruno I site had a fatal flaw: the presence of Holen school and several hundreds of children. But that was where they had decided to construct their base, and that was where the Hoff girls went to school.

Thus, the small community of Laksevåg, thought to be inconsequential to the war effort, became an important strategic pawn in the naval plans of the Germans.

In the meantime, back in the states, the American industrial machine was retooled for wartime production. America had declared war on Japan one day after the bombing of Pearl Harbor on December 7, 1941. In many cases, women entered the blue collar job market for the first time as their men went off to war. Cities began holding scrap metal drives and the government offered bonds to help finance the huge cost of the war.

Air raid wardens were appointed and mock air raids were held to simulate what might happen if an enemy attack should take place. Except for the bombing of Pearl Harbor, none ever did.

As the war years rolled on, the dark days of the Great Depression seemed a distant memory. Jobs became plentiful and the wartime economy shifted into high gear.

But for many civilians, plans were destroyed and extraordinary compromises and hardships were experienced. Families like the Hoffs were split and personal priorities were set aside in deference to the war effort. The future was opened to questions and, regrettably, there were no simple answers. Just more questions.

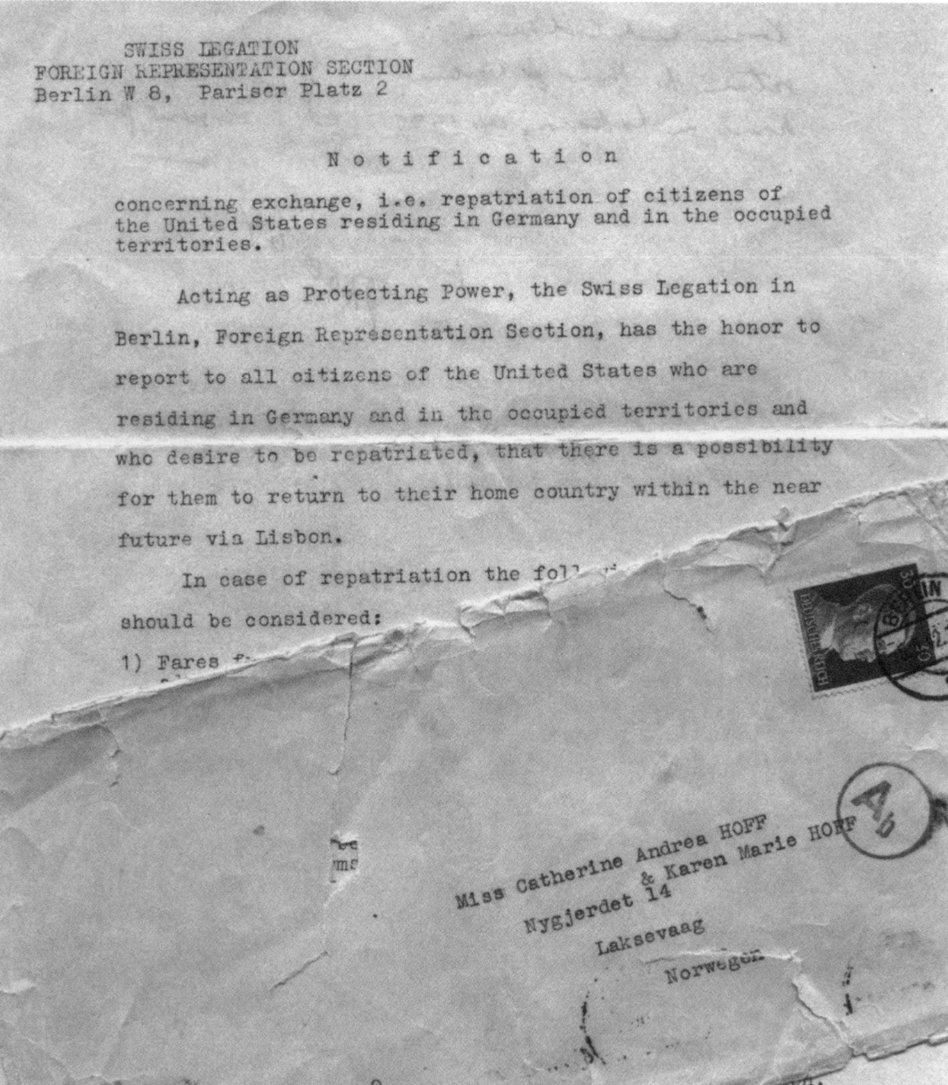
SWISS LEGATION
FOREIGN REPRESENTATION SECTION
Berlin W 8, Pariser Platz 2

N o t i f i c a t i o n

concerning exchange, i.e. repatriation of citizens of the United States residing in Germany and in the occupied territories.

Acting as Protecting Power, the Swiss Legation in Berlin, Foreign Representation Section, has the honor to report to all citizens of the United States who are residing in Germany and in the occupied territories and who desire to be repatriated, that there is a possibility for them to return to their home country within the near future via Lisbon.

In case of repatriation the foll

should be considered:

1) Fares

authorization
incidental expenses
if other funds have not been
provided

5
GERMANS ARRIVE, FREEDOM DEPARTS

In 1940, because of the war, the letters between Mom and Dad encountered periodic stoppages and delays along the way. In spite of the fact that mail deliveries often took about seven weeks, Mom delighted in telling Dad the details of how we were growing up and how we were handling the transition to Norway from the United States. In the few months we had lived in Norway, we quickly adjusted to the language, food, and customs. Also, we made many friends and enjoyed their company, particularly on our outdoor excursions. Of course, Dad was grateful for the information she shared so that he could form a mental picture of us as we matured and changed.

January 3, 1940

I just found out today that the Stavangerfjord *will not be leaving on January 7 as I thought, so I will send you this letter by airmail. I have gotten lots of letters from you, so my spirits are good. How are you, darling? I hope you are the same sweet man I love so much. I am so glad you have decided for sure to come home next summer. The time will not go fast enough for me. I am like a new person when I hear from you and know that you will be coming. The first few months here I felt kind of down but now we can count the months till you are here, so I feel better. I received three air mail letters from you this week. You are so good to me, Calleman.*

Take care, darling, and have a wonderful New Year.

January 5, 1940

My Dear Calle,

Everything is okay. The girls love this wonderful winter weather. There was a group of kids outside playing so Dossi did not come in till 8:30. You should have seen her, all red in her face and smiling from ear to ear and telling me how much fun she'd had. They played the same games her daddy told her he played in Norway as a boy. She remembers how she used to love to sit on your lap and have you tell her stories about Norway. Please take care of yourself, Calle, for you know what you mean to me and the girls. Only five more months and the waiting and writing will be over. The time is not going fast enough for me. These three months we have been apart have been awful, but the worst is over, right Calle? Good night, darling, and don't worry.

January 22, 1940

Hello again, Calle.

It is now 4:30 in the afternoon but the moon is out and it looks beautiful. Karen just came in and said she wants to eat and go to bed. I told her it was too early so I gave her a sandwich for now. I asked her where Dossi is and she said she was skiing. She must have borrowed a pair of skis from somebody. I asked Karen what she would like her daddy to bring her and she said a doll with hair. Well, here comes Dossi and she has been skiing all right. She only fell down twice, she said, and I must have skis, Mor. Maybe next Christmas, I told her.

I have been sitting here reading the paper and it is terrible what goes on in this world. I hope there won't be bad times for us, Calle, now that we are just about to start our lives over. Everything will be fine as long as we are together.

All my love.

Olga

January 31, 1940

Well, Calle,

I am feeling good these days. My spirits are high in spite of everything. I read in the paper that Hitler thinks he is going to win the war. I wish all the countries would get together and get him and Stalin out. The poor Finns, they are trapped and I hope they will soon get help. Many Norwegian families are helping to take care of Finnish children. Well now, January is almost gone and soon it will be your birthday. Just think, Calleman, you will be thirty-seven years old, but we are still young. I will wish you a Happy Birthday now and send one thousand kisses. Take care and don't worry. I love you now and always.

February 5, 1940

I received lots of mail today. Magazines, a book for Dossi, newspaper clippings, and three letters. I love you very much, so please hurry and come home to us. You must come even if you don't have enough money saved. Maybe next winter there will be war here and then it will be impossible to come over. I just hope things will get better and not worse.

Last week, Dossi had fun. School was closed for three days and she went skiing on skis she borrowed from the boy upstairs. She did not want to take time to eat and when she did, she ate with all her clothes on and rushed right back outside. You are going to have a lot of fun with the girls when you come. They speak Norwegian very well now. I had been thinking about asking you to send the game sticks and here they come in your package. For the long winter months it will be a fun game to play. I am going to knit you a sweater and some warm socks for next winter when you are with us. Happy Birthday, Calle. Wish you were here.

February 7, 1940

Today I finally got the letter you had written at Christmas time. I had a good laugh when I read that you now have a zipper in your pants and how it got stuck one day and you couldn't get it unzipped. I am so proud to show everyone your picture. Ingrid is still waiting to hear about a job, but she goes out and sews every day. I have been lucky these last three weeks for I have gotten letters from you every week. You are so good to me, Calleman. When you finally come home I will take good care of you. I dream about that day.

All my love.

February 15, 1940

Well, darling,

We have been apart six months now with three months to go. I can hardly wait to see you. Ingrid and I have decided to go into the business of making hats. I think we can make good money when it becomes known that we make hats. The Bergensfjord *came yesterday, but no mail.*

All my love.

<u>*February 19, 1940*</u>

During the night we had about two feet of snow. Everyone is talking about how much snow we have had this year in Bergen. The most since 1917. The girls love it and have been outside all day. The weather certainly agrees with them for they have real good appetites. Dossi came in and ate five open-faced sandwiches and drank two cups of cocoa. The sun is shining and it makes the snow glisten so it looks beautiful outside.

Take care, Calleman.

<u>*February 26, 1940*</u>

My Dear Calle,

No mail today either, so today is really a Blue Monday for me. Dossi is in school and Karen is sitting here playing with the marbles from the Chinese Checkers game. Last night I was dreaming about you and saw you coming through the door at your Mom and Dad's house. I haven't had a letter for some time now and I am worried about you. Tonight I have been reading some of your old letters. The man whose family lives upstairs from us returned home from the sea. He is not going out to sea again and everyone is happy about that. I was reading the list of shipwrecked seamen from Bergen ships and most of the crew was from Bergen. There was one man from Laksevåg and he lived next door to us. They have a little girl who comes to visit us and the other day she told me she didn't have a Daddy any more.

Love,

Olga and the Girls

February 27, 1940

Happy Birthday to you, my darling.

How are you, Calle? I think about you day and night. It has been raining so hard today, the worst I have seen since we came home. Well now, February is gone too. The time is going faster now, don't you think Calle? Soon you will be here. I told the girls it was your birthday today and Karen asked me if I was going to bake you a cake. That was the first thing she thought about. Dossi came in looking like she had taken a bath with her clothes on for it was raining so hard, but she thought it was fun. Our girls are fine and healthy, Calle, and you will be proud of them. Well, darling, I must stop for tonight. I hope you are the same sweet man I love so much. Take care for now.

Love,

Olga, Dossi, and Karen

March 6, 1940

Hello Calleman,

It was good to hear in your letter that you are fine and the same sweet boy as always. When you can afford it you must buy yourself a new blue suit with two pairs of pants. It must be nice now to have zippers in your pants. You are going to look so good when you come.

Dossi will be so proud to have her Daddy here and Karen will probably talk a blue streak. That time cannot come fast enough for me.

Love,

Olga

March 10, 1940

It's nine o'clock Sunday night. The girls are sleeping and we are all fine. I both cry and laugh when I read your letters. I am so proud to have a man like you love me so much. I love you as much and it hurts when I can't do for you all the things I want to do. It has been seven months now, darling, so we must get back together as soon as we can. I don't know how we have stood it this long, but we have to believe that it will be over soon. I live from letter to letter, Calle, and think about all of us being together soon. The girls will be very happy to have their daddy back as well.

Love,

Olga

April 7, 1940

Hello, darling,

How are you? I got a lot of mail yesterday, Calle. You will laugh when I tell you what happened. The mailman always rings two small rings when he comes. I was on the floor cleaning when he came and as I got up in a hurry I bumped my head on the cupboard door that I had left open and almost fell in the wash bucket. Then I hurt my leg and was almost an invalid by the time I got to the door. I soon forgot about that when I saw all the mail. I love you and will write again soon.

This was the last letter Mom wrote before the Germans invaded Norway on April 9, 1940. When we awoke that morning, we could hear the sounds of troops marching in the streets. They were making their presence known as dramatically as they could. Though we didn't yet know what was happening, we soon learned the grim news.

Within days the German soldiers had come into our homes and had taken whatever they wanted, including food, blankets, and other personal property. They were particularly interested in liberating us from any news on the war by removing all radios found in our homes.

They dropped propaganda leaflets from airplanes telling us that they didn't intend to take over Norway but instead wanted to protect the Scandinavian countries from becoming a battleground for the British. The leaflets went on to say that, "Under the circumstances, it is important for the Norwegian king's government and the German government to work together freely and without interruption."

They concluded with a direct order to the Norwegian people to "work together and not give the Germans any resistance." Everyone was told to continue with their lives as normal.

"From now on, the Germans will protect the Norwegian people," the Nazis proclaimed. As we all know, that was not true.

After the invasion, all correspondence from Norway to other parts of Europe and the world was halted. By the middle of May, 1940, correspondence was allowed to resume, but all letters between America and Norway were opened and inspected by the Germans. Since telegrams by private citizens were not allowed, Mom experienced sleepless nights for several weeks over her inability to let Dad know that we were okay.

She also realized that Dad's return to Norway might be postponed because of the invasion, so she began trying to obtain the necessary documentation that would enable her to take us back to America.

The Hoff family in Norway saw the situation in a different light. They still wanted Dad to leave his job at Pontiac Motors and find a way to come to Norway, where they were sure he would be able to find work.

The parents on both sides of the family were aging and hadn't seen Dad in a number of years. Of course, his brothers and sisters were anxious to have him back as well. Ignoring the potential opposition to her strategy regarding her proposed return to America, Mom moved persistently to get her paperwork in order so that the three of us could leave at the earliest opportunity.

In the meantime, on the day of the invasion, Mom, Karen, and I went to the country to our grandparents' home and stayed there all summer, out of harm's way. We were glad to be out of the city, as the German presence was like the all-consuming fog that settles in from the sea. They ordered around any non-German in their presence and forced local civilians to work in menial jobs for them.

Tante Ingrid did not join us. She stayed in town to take care of Bestefar and to look for work. She had been laid off from Sundt's as the rationing of fabrics began and business declined. She and Mom planned to start their own hat business, but that did not fare well for the same reason. The war had officially come to Norway, and we were feeling its effects.

All of Mom's letters after this point show her increasing fears and frustrations that our family was not coming back together as quickly as she had planned, and they describe some of her anxieties and concerns.

May 14, 1940

How are you? You can believe I have had many sleepless nights since the invasion on April 9. It does not matter so much for me, Calle, it is worse for you since you are so far away and have to hear all the stories going around. We are all fine, Calleman, and all is okay so far. We left town the same day the Germans came and went to the country with your mom and dad and we are still here.

The first week the English bombed the German ships that lay in Puddefjorden. The English and French planes come once in a while and bomb German targets around town. You know we are safe here in the country. I tried to send you a telegram last Friday so I hope you got it. We have been forbidden to send mail out, for I have tried several times but with no luck. However, I saw in the paper yesterday that we can now send mail but by airmail only.

I love you, Calle.

Olga

May 23, 1940

My dear husband,

I am so glad we can exchange letters again. I got your letter today but could not believe what I was reading. Calle, do you really think this war is going to last till 1945? That can't be possible. I just hope we can still write to each other. I live for your letters. Roosevelt is going to give a speech on the radio on May 27 and we are all anxious to hear what he has to say. Will America go to war or not?

<u>*May 26, 1940*</u>

I got your telegram last Wednesday. I know you are not able to send any money now, but don't worry. We are managing. I am getting help from the government. I get 25 kroner every ten days and I get along fine with that up here in the country. The telegram I tried to send you on May 7 did not go through. I was just notified that we are not allowed to send telegrams. The girls are fine and enjoying the country. Dossi asked me if there is war in America. I told her no and she was happy about that. I wish I could let you know we are okay.*

Love,
Olga

<u>*June 6, 1940*</u>

We are all fine, Calle. Yesterday was Dossi's birthday and we had cake and hot chocolate. I wish you could have been here with us. The American Consulate has promised me they will notify you that we are okay. Next week your Mom and Dad will move up here to the country for good, and they want me to stay here with them. I think it will be okay to go back to town. The German soldiers seem well behaved, so please don't worry.

*Mom never fully explained the help she received from the government; all we know is that there was some sort of aid provided to mothers alone with children.

June 12, 1940

Hello, darling.

I was so surprised and happy to get a letter from you today, and I am so glad to hear that you are okay. As long as we can write to each other we will be fine. We will have the rest of our lives to be together when this is over so we can't give up.

I did get the 100 kroner you sent. I think I wrote that to you before the war. It was in the same letter that I sent the pictures. The banks have been closed since the Germans invaded, so I had a hard time for a while. Then I got some help from the government. The hat business is not going the way we thought it would. Right now people are not too interested in hats. There must be a solution to this war soon.

June 16, 1940

Are you getting my letters, Calle? I am so anxious to hear if they are getting through. I was happy and surprised when I got two letters from you this week. We are all fine as always. I am so mad at myself, for I sent you a telegram asking you to send some money. I just found out you are not allowed to send money, so now you will be worried. I am getting help so we are doing fine. Please don't worry.

In your letter you asked if I want to come back to America. I can get passage and pay for it when we get to New York, but I am afraid to travel during these times. I think we will wait and see what happens and be patient and safe a while longer. What do you think, Calle? Maybe you should think about coming home here. Your mom and dad have been looking forward to seeing you again.

I read in the paper that we can send messages through the Red Cross. I hope you have gotten my letters and that the Consulate sent you the telegram they promised to send. I hope you are feeling better, Calle, now that we can write to each other again.

July 5, 1940

How are you these days, Calleman? We are all okay. Once in a while some English planes come over and drop bombs. Nordness was in flames the other night. 105 homes burned to the ground. Alf Madsen's parents' house was hit and they could not save anything but themselves. There are so many people homeless. The girls and I will stay here in the country as long as we have to so don't worry, darling.

July 13, 1940

Dear Calle,

I am waiting for a letter from you, darling. A week from today is my birthday and I hope I hear from you by that time, or maybe you can send a telegram. I have been so depressed this week that I am ashamed of myself. I know it is worse for you, Calle.

Thursday is payday. I get along fine on the money I get from the state. It does not buy any extras, but we have enough for food and necessities.

What are you up to these days? I have been reading all the letters you sent over again, even the one with fifty pages. I hope you are feeling better now than you did when the war first broke out. If only I knew if you have received any of my letters. It is so awful not knowing, but I am sure that by next weekend I will hear from you.

It is wonderful weather we are having these days. The moon is shining in my window as I sit here. Good night for now, darling.

July 14, 1940

Today I am happier than I have been in a long time. I got a letter from you today and I was so happy to hear that you had gotten a couple of my letters. I was also happy to hear that you were taking a trip to New York. You certainly need a vacation after all you have been through. I'm sure it feels good to get away a little and talk to different people. Your loving Olga

July 29, 1940

I spent the whole week in town. You know, Calle, we have to move for we cannot afford to keep the apartment any longer. We are moving to the basement apartment in the same house. We will just have two rooms now and a kitchen but it will be fine. My dad will have his own room and the four of us will share the other room. It will only cost forty-five kroner a month. We will stay in the country for a while yet. Take care, Calleman, and don't worry.

August 2, 1940

My own dear Calle, I got a letter from you again yesterday and you won't believe how happy that made me. I did not expect another letter from New York, for I know how hard it is to write when you are visiting people. You look so stylish in the picture you sent, like a real American. Dossi smiled all over her face when she saw the picture and said, "Isn't Daddy fine, Mor?" Karen said she could not remember you having such fine shoes, so I had to explain to her that you had bought new shoes since we left.

August 11, 1940

How are things with you, Calleman? Our girls are growing big and healthy. Karen is so pretty and so round in her face. Dossi is pretty too, but she is so thin. We can be proud of them, Calle. Please don't worry that they will forget you, for we talk about you all the time. No, darling, they will not forget their daddy.

With love from the three of us,

Olga, Dossi, and Karen

August 23, 1940

Well, Calleman, here we are back in the city and all is fine. Dossi started school last week. She is proud to be in the second grade. She is sitting here knitting and I wish you could see her. Her tongue moves as fast as her hands. You would get a good laugh. Karen has gotten big and tall. Everyone says she still looks like her daddy. Dossi looks like herself. No one knows who she looks like, but she sure is ours with the help of Dr. Green, right, Calle?

I have been busy this week, Calle. I have made and sold four hats, a child's coat and dress, and more work is waiting. It feels good to be making money again. Ingrid is still working at Teffre's, so we will get along fine this winter.

Well, darling, I will have to stop for now. A thousand hugs and kisses from all three of us. Please don't worry, as we are fine.

September 18, 1940

My Dear Calleman,

It is about midnight but I must write you a few words. Both Dossi and I got a letter from you today and it sure made us happy. Karen was so disappointed for she did not get a letter. I tried to explain to her that Dossi's letter was for her, too. She was not satisfied with that for she wants her name on the envelope. We love the pictures you sent. You look so sweet standing there smiling at us. If we could only be together again either here or there, as long as we are all together.

Calle, I got an answer from the Consulate in Oslo yesterday and they said you must write the Department of Justice in Washington on my behalf regarding my status. You should also go to the immigration office in your area and fill out form #633 from the Department of Justice and send it to Washington. Then if everything is in order they will send it to the Consulate here. Since you are an American citizen I have the right to ask for a non quota immigration visa. Since the girls have American passports, all I have to do for them is have new pictures taken.

Lots of love to you, darling, from all three of us.

September 24, 1940

My dear Calleman,

I hope you got the card I sent last Saturday telling you we have gotten the money you sent. You must have been surprised to get a telegram from the Consulate, and maybe more surprised that the money had to be sent in the girls' names. It had to be that way, Calle, as they are American citizens. I hope you understand, darling. I do not want you to think there is something wrong. You do not have to send any more money. If we really need it I will tell you. We are sewing and making hats for many people, so the time goes fast.

The girls and I have been in town all afternoon shopping for things we need. The girls got new boots, so now Karen's feet won't freeze like they did last year. Your mom has knitted them warm wool socks and mittens with the yarn I sent her. They also got some warm underwear, so don't worry about them. Thank you for the money so I could get these things for the girls. I got 653 kroner for the dollars you sent and I will be very careful with the money. I bought film today so I can take pictures of the girls on the next sunny day to send to you. It is 12:30 at night now, darling, so I will say good night. Don't worry.

Your loving Olga

<u>October 24, 1940</u>

Just a few words to let you know we are fine and we had lots of mail today. The girls got their coloring books and paint which they are very happy over. The girls are so grateful for everything they get; they are not spoiled, Calle. I am happy to hear that you are well. I love you, dear, and don't worry.

November 4, 1940

The days, weeks, and years go by, Calleman. This war will surely end soon and we will be back together. It is no good living this way, darling, for the girls and I need you as you need us. Karen has become a real nice girl. She wishes she could write to you. Dossi is writing to you right now and she promised Karen she would write her name at the bottom, too. I am sitting here looking at the colored picture you sent. I wish I could reach out and hug you for you look so wonderful. If only I hadn't left, Calle, but we didn't know this would happen. We are fine and healthy and have our letters which is something to be grateful for. God knows I miss you so much but we must be strong for the girls' sake. Sometimes I feel so hopeless. I have to think that each day that passes brings us closer together.

November 20, 1940

How are you, darling?

My dad has been sick so he went to the doctor and found out that he has pneumonia. He is not very strong and has been sick a lot these past years. We are hoping he will be well soon. You thought Karen had changed so much from the pictures I sent you. I think so, too, and I see her every day. She still looks like you, especially in the eyes. I am anxious to hear if you got those papers in order for me. I am sorry you had to take half a day off from work to go to Detroit to do that. I asked if it would have been easier if I had gotten a reentry permit when we first came, but the man said it would not have made any difference, for things are different now. I still have not heard about the girls' passports. I don't know when we will be able to come, but it is best to have everything in order. Since the mail takes so long we will wish you a Merry Christmas now, and I hope we will be together in the new year.

All my love,

Olga

<u>*November 22, 1940*</u>

Hello, darling,

I was late getting to bed but even later getting to sleep for I lay awake thinking about my papers. Since our girls are American citizens, couldn't they let us come back? I have to hope that it will all work out. It has been three months now since I have heard from the Consulate. I love you, darling, and don't worry about us and have a wonderful Christmas. I know it is worse for you than for me for I have the girls with me. I cry for you, Calle, when I read your letters. We must stay strong, Calleman, and you must believe we are fine.

<u>*December 1, 1940*</u>

Well, now we have started the Christmas month. I hope things will turn out okay for us. Have you heard anything from Washington? Won't it be wonderful to be together again? I don't know how I had the heart to come without you, but it was done with good intentions. When we finally get together I will take good care of you in every way, and we will have the rest of our lives to be happy. The girls will have a lot to tell their daddy. You will get a good laugh out of them. Karen is smart, Calle, she can write her name and knit. We laugh at her often when she is sitting on the floor knitting with her legs crossed and looking like an old lady.

I will close for now, darling.

December 18, 1940

Hello, Calle,

I had two letters from you today and one was so long it took me three hours to read it. I will read it again tonight. Dossi has made Christmas tree decorations with colored paper at school and they look pretty good. On Wednesday the girls will dance around the Christmas tree at school and Dossi will get her report card.

Good night for now, Calleman.

December 26, 1940

Tomorrow our baby girl will be five years old. She invited all the kids in the neighborhood and all the family for her birthday. I have ordered a cream cake from the bakery with pink roses on it and it will say "Happy Birthday, Karen." The birthday card she got from you a while ago she has to show to everyone. It is cold here in the apartment. I would like to move from here so the girls could have their own room instead of all of us sharing this one room. It would be better for them. I won't have much sewing to do anymore for all material has been rationed and what we can get is very expensive.

So long till tomorrow, my darling.

December 28, 1940

Dear Calleman,

I have not had much time to write these last few days. I have to get things ready for Christmas, but you are always on my mind. You know everything has to be clean for Christmas. The weather has been beautiful all week and the girls have had a lot of fun at the new park. They are outside from morning till night. Christmas Eve was beautiful, cold and clear and a full Christmas moon. We got the Pinnekjøtt at three o'clock. The girls got all dressed up and waited patiently to open their gifts. They could see Santa had been here for there were a lot of presents for them under the tree. The doorbell rang and guess what, Calle? Your telegram came and we were so happy and surprised. I had to take a deep breath so I would not cry. We had a wonderful dinner and there would have been plenty for you. I could not get you out of my mind all night, Calle, and I was hoping you were not depressed this Christmas Eve. Next Christmas will be better, darling. The girls were anxious to open their presents. No one was more surprised than I to get a package from you. Thank you for the beautiful robe and sweater. You are wonderful, Calle, for you think of everything and it always makes me happy. It seems I don't do enough for you, darling, but as soon as we are back together again, I will do everything for you.*

*Pinnekjøtt is salted and dried ribs of mutton, a traditional Christmas meat in Norway.

December 31, 1940

Hello, darling.

Well, now it is New Year's Eve and we are still apart. It is eleven o'clock and the girls are sound asleep. They stayed up late and played sticks and Chinese Checkers with their Bestefar. Alf Madsen thinks by next Christmas you will be here with us. I hope he is right. Good night, Calleman

And so 1940 ended, with Mom and Dad and us girls still separated. Sixteen months had passed since we had last seen one another, but little did we know that nearly another five whole years would go by before we would be back together again.

6
A PAINFUL SEPARATION

As 1941 began, Mom was ready to take us back to America if the travel documents needed for passage could be obtained quickly. Speed was important because the war was becoming more and more threatening. If America became directly involved, even more restrictions on travel might arise.

In her letters, Mom begins to show signs of her desperation and the critical need she feels to be with Dad. His letters to her express this same longing.

January 4, 1941

My Dear Calleman,

Today I got a letter from you, darling. It has been exactly four weeks today since the last one. When a letter comes the girls want to know what you said and are you coming soon or are we going back to America. They have not forgotten their daddy. Dossi asks so often, "What time is it in America?" and "What is Daddy doing?" or "Is he working now?" Just think, Calle, it has been almost two years.

January 14, 1941

Hello again, darling. I got some work Saturday morning that had to be finished by today so my writing was delayed. It will be hard to get work now for material is rationed, but I hope I get some so I can earn some money. The kids and I have enough clothes so don't worry about that. Well, Calle, everything must come to an end, and so must this war also. I wish I could get an American newspaper so I could read what people in Europe think about the war.

Calle, you must remember to buy the Life *magazines and save them all for me so I can see what has happened. I'm glad I have our atlas so I can follow along. I am so tired of these black window shades. Well, Calle, I hope this finds you well and healthy and in a good mood.*

Love to you from us all.

Olga, Dossi, and Karen

February 8, 1941

Good morning, Calle.

It is just nine o'clock and the girls are still in bed. They are sitting in their beds playing. Dossi does not have to be in school until twelve o'clock today. We were surprised to see how much it had snowed during the night. Dossi wants to go out and ski. She said to say hello to you and Karen said from her, too. Well, Calleman, take care of yourself. I got some sewing this week so I will earn a little money. Don't worry about us.

Love,

Olga

February 14, 1941

My dear Calleman,

I have had a busy week with washing, cleaning, and sewing. Best of all, I got a letter from you today and last Monday I got two letters. I will take a trip up to the Consulate today to see what they have to say. I doubt they will say anything for they said they would let me know when they hear anything from Washington.

I am so glad you liked the pictures of the girls, Calle. There is such a big difference in Karen since two years ago. When she sees the mailman out on the street, she asks him if he has a letter from her Far today. If he does, she is so proud to bring it home and she wants to open it. She is so much like you in her eyes, Calle. Can you see that in the pictures?

We will have such a good time, Calle, when you and I and the girls are together. We don't have it so bad here, Calle. We don't see too much of the war and we have enough to eat. We have plenty of milk, potatoes, and bread, so don't believe it if you hear we are all starving. We have much to be thankful for as long as we are healthy.

We love you, the kids and I, so take care of yourself.

Olga

<u>February 19, 1941</u>

Calle,

I was so glad to get your letter today and to know that you have heard from Washington and that they said we can come back to America. It is going to work out for us after all. Tuesday I went to the Consulate but they were closed for the day. I will talk to the Consulate about the best way to travel. What a time this has been, Calle, with so many tears and feeling so helpless so many times. I am so happy for this news, darling.

Good night.

<u>*March 1, 1941*</u>

I finally got that letter from Oslo so I went right away to the Consulate with it. He said all is okay from the American side and now it is just a matter of getting out of here. On Monday I will have to go to the front office and talk to them about leaving. I am like a new person since we heard from Washington, even though I went to the travel office and they said it would take at least a month and a half to get my travel permits for they have to go to Berlin and back. It will cost $250.00 for me and half of that for the girls. That is so much money, Calle. Then we have the long train ride to Berlin and then we have to fly to Lisbon, Portugal and from there to New York.

Well, Calle, I will have to stop for now.

<u>*April 2, 1941*</u>

My darling,

I have everything in order now except our permit to leave. I talked with the Consulate today about leaving Norway and he advised me not to go at this time. Even if I get permission he said he is sure you would not want us to leave. That you would rather have us alive in Norway than take a chance on traveling such a dangerous route. Everyone here thinks I am crazy to even think about leaving. Calleman, do you think the man at the Consulate is right? The route over Moscow is totally closed now so I guess we have to wait and see what happens. I am glad all our papers are in order so we are ready to go when the time comes. I know you are as disappointed as I am, Calleman, but I don't know what else to do. We have to be strong for the girls' sake.

May 14, 1941

I got a letter from you today and I'm happy to hear you are okay, but disappointed that we can't come now. I got a notice that the girls can leave but not me. There is no way I would send our two little girls out in this world alone.

July 1, 1941

How are things with you, my darling? We are all fine. Summer is here and we have been in the country for a week now. It was wonderful to get out of town for a little while. Your mom wants us to stay the whole summer, but I feel like I have to get back to town to work. I hope America does not go to war. It will be awful if we can't write to each other. Don't feel sad, Calle, for we will overcome this.

July 5, 1941

My dear husband,

I did not get to write to you yesterday for I had work to do. I listened to President Roosevelt yesterday on your Dad's radio and it sounds like America is getting involved in the war. It was good to hear his voice again; it was just like I was there in America. He was on a London station and it was very clear and we could hear every word, even out here in the country. I know you can't send us any money, but don't worry for I will earn enough.*

Love,

Olga, Dossi, and Karen

*Even though radios had been confiscated and, in fact, it was illegal for a Norwegian to have a radio in his or her home, it was fairly easy to hide them out in the country since the Germans spent little time there.

August 20, 1941

Good morning, darling.

I just got a letter from you and I am so sorry you feel so depressed, which puts me in a bad mood. I know it is much worse for you being all alone, but please, darling, take care and don't worry. These are tough times, Calle, but we must not make it worse by letting it get us down. I know there is nothing to be happy about, but we should be grateful that we are all alive. Don't be afraid for us, Calle, for we are fine. Please do everything you can to be in a better mood. Karen has gotten her first new tooth.

I will write again soon.

December 2, 1941

My dear husband,

I was so happy yesterday morning when two letters came from you. I am glad to hear that you finally got word about the money and I know you were also glad to hear how it has helped me this winter. Karen and I were in town yesterday while Dossi was in school. I bought some material to make some dresses for the girls. I told them it would be their Christmas present from me and daddy. I had to say something, Calle, so I told them you had said they must have new dresses for Christmas.

You said that you would like to send me some pounds of coffee. Some people are getting coffee from America. I understand there is coffee in Portugal and that people in America can send money and our address here and the company will send the coffee to us. I don't know how true it is but that's what I have heard.

They were in full swing at Sundt's putting up Christmas decorations, so Karen and I walked around and looked at everything. With the blackout there will not be any decorations outside.

Have a Merry Christmas, Calle. We are all fine and well and miss you.

Love,

Olga, Dossi, and Karen

At this point, all correspondence between Mom and Dad came to a complete halt because the U.S. declared war on Japan after the Pearl Harbor attack. So for the next 3½ years, the only communication between them was a few words written through the Red Cross agency. These messages, however, took several months, but were eventually received.

Even though Dad couldn't send any regular mail to us, he continued to write us cards and letters. It was his way of talking to us, of trying to keep himself from losing all faith that he would ever see us again.

The first few messages that follow are some of the Red Cross notes:

February 3, 1942

Happy Birthday Calle. We are all fine, don't worry. Hope you are OK. Waiting for you. Love Olga.

March 4, 1944

My Dear Wife,

How are you, Catherine and Karen? I have not heard from you in a long time. I'm worried. I'm fine. Love, Carl

February 17, 1942

Calle, Hope to hear from you soon. All is well. The girls are fine. Are you alright? Love Olga, Catherine and Karen

December 21, 1942

To my little girl. Daddy is very lonesome without you. Happy Birthday. How are Catherine and Mother? Hope to see you soon. Love Daddy

April 30, 1942

My Dear Man. We are all fine. Are you OK Calle? We long to hear from you. Olga, Catherine and Karen

December 1, 1942

My Dear Wife. We are crossing through some hard times just now, but a few words from you would do wonders. Love Carl

March 9, 1943

Everything is fine. Thinking about you all the time. We are well. Love yours, Olga, Catherine and Karen

September 7, 1943

My Dear, I am fine too. Say hello to Mother and Dad. Merry Christmas to you all. Hope to see you soon. Love as always Carl

November 2, 1943

Today is our anniversary Calle. I hope we are together for our next anniversary. The girls and I talk about you all the time. Olga, Catherine and Karen

June 5, 1944

Happy Birthday to you Catherine. I am glad to hear you are all OK. I am fine. Love Daddy

To help keep his loneliness in check, Dad also wrote us long, newsy letters that indicated the depth of his despair at times, as well as his attempts to keep his spirits up.

September 17, 1943

Hello Olga, how are you and the little ones doing? Are you getting enough to eat? When I am working at night I think about you and the girls and what they will think of their daddy. They will probably not remember me, but we will get reacquainted soon enough. I feel good when I think about you and me together. You will have it good from your Calleman one fine day. We will take back these years.
Love,
Carl

September 21, 1943

My dear Olga and girls,
On Monday I went to the Red Cross to send you a few

words. They know me pretty well down there now. The nurses sit and have a good laugh and say "Another message, Mr. Hoff?" There have been a lot of films shown here lately about Norway, so they are always interested when I talk about Norway. I feel fine, so when I left there I took a walk down Saginaw Street and met many friends I have not seen for a while. I have been cutting things out of the newspaper that we will read together one of these days. This is a strange war. Hitler will get his in the near future. I was reading some old letters that I had written and I see I predicted that the war would last to 1945. I was not sure at that time, but it looks like I was not far off. Olga, what a day it will be for us when it is finally over.

September 22,1943

Hello, Madame,

By rights I should be sleeping but it is one of those days when thinking about you has gotten the best of me. No matter how much I toss and turn I am always there with you. It is hell lying there like that. Thinking about you and seeing you and the kids in my mind's eye and then realizing you are a thousand miles away from me. Seeing my girls and wanting to hold them in my arms and give them care and love like a daddy should. I wonder when that day will come, Olga? Boy oh boy, what a fix we got ourselves into. Well, Olga, goodbye for now. I'd better start building my rowboat. I tell the boys at work I wore out ten pairs of oars coming over here but that I will need twelve pairs going back for it is all uphill!

(later that same day)

I had a good sleep now, Olga. I have been listening to the radio for a while, but now it is almost time to go to work. I am working on guns these days. [Dad worked nights and worked on the line which made guns rather than cars during the wartime years.] I feel that each gun that is finished and leaves here brings me closer to the day we will be together. I am always thinking of you. We will have it good one of these days, just you, me, and the girls.

Love,

Carl

September 23, 1943

My Olga,

I'm fantasizing about the day when we will be together again. If I come home, I will take the Swedish line to Gøteborg in Sweden. You could meet me there and we could have several days together alone. Although it is only a thought and a dream, I feel so good about the possibility of being with you once again.

I will treat you like a queen, Olga, and we will take back these years. When we meet in Gøteborg, I will kiss you on the mouth, for we will be strangers to everyone else there. We will snuggle up in the finest hotel with all the trimmings. How does that make you feel, Olga?

September 24, 1943

Hello, Madame Hoff,

Here I am again. The weather is still good but a little fallish. The leaves are starting to turn a little. Just like me, since my hair is starting to get a little gray, but I am told I still look young. I am taking good care of myself so I will be strong and healthy when you come home. I bought an extra hundred dollars in war bonds this month. The saying is it will take a lot of bullets and war bonds to beat Hitler, so I am trying to do my share. I want this war over as soon as possible. Well, Olga, I only hope to find you and the girls alive when this is all over. Until then, goodbye. Say hello to the girls.

Love,
Calleman

September 26, 1943

My dear wife,

Do you feel as I do sometimes that no matter how many people you have around you you feel all alone in this world? I just wait, think, and dream about the day I will see my family again. The days, weeks, and years go by and I work, think, and dream over and over again about you, Karen, and Dossi. Just think, it has been over four years now since we have seen each other so now it can't be much longer till our dreams come true. Well, otherwise I am fine so don't worry, dear. I bought Karen another $50.00 bond so now they have two each. This way they will have some money when they

grow up and get married. I am sure they wonder by now what I look like. If we could only write to each other. There are so many things I wonder about. The war goes on and I am one day closer to you and the little ones. Maybe I will see you in the spring.

Love,

Carl

September 29, 1943

My dear wife,

I didn't sleep well today. I have this war on my mind constantly. I was dreaming I was in Bergen with you today and we went to buy some fish. I saw everything so clearly. I miss you and love you. You know, Madame, Calle is waiting for you. I think about you and how good it will be to be with each other again. It will probably be like the first time we kissed in Rådalen. Do you remember? When you and I were seventeen, and life and love were new. I am smiling now just thinking about those days.

I have been sitting here clipping articles out of the newspaper, but that gets tiresome. The war goes on but we are winning, Olga, so that gives me hope. I wonder how Germany can hold out. It is not going well for Hitler in Russia, and he has nothing to be proud of in Italy. It won't be too long before we are in Rome, but we have a long way to go before we get to Berlin.

I can sing now about how nice you will be to come home to.

Your loving Calle

<u>*September 30, 1943*</u>

Today is Thursday and here I am again. I don't know how I can express myself to you today so that you can understand. I have a sense of something very near trying to lay hands on me. Something or someone is seeking to make itself seen, heard, and felt. I don't understand it myself. My eyes are dim, Olga, and my ears dull. I feel depressed but I will never lose hope. I will go down if I lose hope, Olga. It is this damn war. There will come a day when the curtain of this world war drama will come down, and it may happen all of a sudden.

<u>*October 4, 1943*</u>

My Dear Madame Hoff,

It is Sunday today and I am taking it easy. I went to the German Mills last night and met a lot of friends. Pederson and Olson were among them. I wanted to dance but I did not ask anyone for I want to wait till I can hold you in my arms. We are going to have ourselves a good polka one day, Olga. The way they dance nowadays is strange. They call it "cutting a rug." It is only three o'clock in the afternoon but I think I will get dressed and go to Pontiac for a while. How are you and the girls doing, Olga? You will be so nice to come home to.

October 5, 1943

My Dear Olga, Catherine and Karen,

Time goes and here I am again. I did not feel so good yesterday. I guess it was the Monday Blues. All kinds of things go through my mind when I am not feeling well. Just think if something were to happen to me and we would never see each other again. Today I feel fine. I go with you in my mind Olga all the time and I am sure it is the same with you. This is an awful way to live, but the lights of yesterday will shine again. Once again they will speak to our hearts of happiness, of family life, of friendly meals, simple past times and laughter. I hope Catherine and Karen don't feel the loneliness you and I feel and the homesickness for days gone by. Some day the darkness will be lifted, the war and blackouts too.

You and the kids are dear to me as ever. It will be a happy day when we can send letters to each other again. I sent a few words to you yesterday by Red Cross. The ladies at the Red Cross office all say, "Hello, Mr. Hoff, another one?" They all know me by name, so I guess I am their best customer. Well Olga, this is all for today. I hope we live to see the day we are hoping for.

Love to you all,

Carl

October 11, 1943

My dear Olga,

I am down in the dumps. I guess there is nothing wrong with feeling that way at times as we miss each other so much and we are depressed about the world events that are keeping us apart. Well, it is a fine night tonight with a full moon. It's like the night sky is dancing around me as I sit here by the window. Through the open lonely door I seem to hear the footsteps and voices of you and the kids as if it were yesterday. I hear the sobs and sorrow you feel. I feel your arms around me and your tears and kisses, too. I hear the kids crying and laughing. I wonder, Olga, if tonight you and the kids will say a prayer just for Daddy, that I will see you all again soon and that you will all be away from the war. God knows if there were something I could do I would do it. I am sitting here with tears running down my face, Olga, for that's the way I feel. There will come a day when you will stand in front of me and we will welcome each other home from these terrible years. What a day that will be. I must pull myself together now and go to work.

Love to you all,

Calle

October 13, 1943

This is a strange war, Olga. Something big is going to happen soon, but I don't know what it is. It is in the air, I

can feel it. We have got to win this war. Do you remember this song? "Every cloud must have a silver lining. Wait until the sun shines through, and come to me my melancholy baby, cuddle up and don't be blue. All your fears are foolish fancy." That's all I can remember. I am sure you will know the tune or else you can wait and Dossi and I will sing it for you. We used to be good at singing together. How is Karen doing? Does she have a good singing voice? Well, this is all for now, Olga. You will be so nice to come home to. Love to you all.

As always,
Your lonesome Calle

October 16, 1943

Hello, Madame Hoff,

I am happy for each day that I feel good and can sit here alone with my thoughts of you and the girls. I have pulled myself together and am trying to look at the bright side of things. It is not bad when I am working, but the evenings are cruel. I like turning on the radio and hearing the music we used to love, but when I turn it off I start thinking about all those times. I wish we were back there, you and I. I am filled with new hope, Olga. Dear God, make it the same for you. You and the kids are everything in the world to me.

Love,
Calle

October 20, 1943

Hello Olga,

I have been thinking and wondering how this will all turn out. I know we get depressed sometimes, but I am clinging to my dreams, for peace will come. Have faith, they tell me, but it is very hard sometimes. I will make it, for when I come home to you I will bring my dreams and we will soon forget all the horrors we have known. Christmas is getting close again, Olga. I don't want to think about it. I go and buy things for the girls once in a while so they will have something from their daddy someday when this war is over. I often wonder how my girls are doing, how they look, and how big they are getting. I can't wait to put my arms around them and you. Say hello to them from me. You will be so nice to come home to one day.

Your loving Calle

October 24, 1943

Hello again, Madame Hoff.

I am sitting here waiting for dinner and then I will go to a show. I hope I can get in for there are a lot of people going to shows these days for that is the only entertainment we have. Sonja Henie is playing at the Oakland, so that's what I want to see. I have been thinking about the fun-filled Sundays we used to have. What a day it will be when I have the three of you here again. The war goes on, but each day

brings us closer together. I feel so bad that my girls have to go through all of this. They will have it good when they are with their daddy again. I will be so glad when I can send you these letters. I think you are waiting to hear how much I love you and miss you. You and I have always been one since our school days. Do you remember this song? "I want a girl just like the girl that married dear old dad." In other words, we will be together forever. In 1944 I am sure we will be together under the same roof. I hope we have the strength to hold on till then.

Love and kisses,
Calleman

<u>October 25, 1943</u>

My Dear Olga, Catherine, and Karen,

Olga, Olga, I am having one of those blue Mondays. I have had that feeling all day. I went to Pontiac for a while, but it did not help. I bought you and the girls some cards and came home to write them. It is as though I want to sleep all the time so I don't have to think about everything. It is getting close to November 2, our fourteenth wedding anniversary. I would like to relive the first ten years and forget about these last few. We will have to keep our spirits up a little while longer. Thinking about you and my girls is all that is keeping me together these days. It is hell what we are going through, Olga, but we will be together again one day. I wish we could write to each other. I want to hear more about

my girls. I am very proud of them and I know they feel the same about me. There will come a day, dear, and as always you will be so nice to come home to, you Olga and my two darlings. If not this Christmas for sure next Christmas. I am sitting here thinking about you and I can almost feel you right here. You, Dossi, and Tiny [Karen] mean everything to me.

Love to you all,

Calle

October 26, 1943

Hello, Karen,

Once upon a time, I had a little girl like you. But now I am all alone in this world. Someday Daddy will come back to you and Mommy. I have to win this war first.

Love to you from Daddy.

October 29, 1943

Hello Dear,

I don't know why, Olga, but I feel sick, or is it just that I miss you so much? I hope you are all okay. I feel so nervous and shaky today that I can hardly write. I went to bed for a while and tried to sleep, but it did not help. If I could only hear from you. It is terrible to live this way, Olga. I only have one thing on my mind and that is for this war to be over so I

can see all of you. I want you to know I love you more than ever. I miss you, dear.

Love to you all,

Calle

November 2, 1943

My dear Olga,

I remember this day so well fourteen years ago. We were so proud to walk down the aisle in church hand in hand. Now here we are thousands of miles apart, but we are still as much in love as ever. It is so sad to think back and I get so mad at myself for deciding we should do what we did. Having you and the girls leave was the biggest mistake of my life. We have missed out on so much. Well, it's too late to worry about that now so we have to make the best of it and keep looking for the light at the end of the tunnel. I am hoping this will be the last anniversary we are apart.

I went to the Red Cross office and sent you an anniversary greeting. I wrote, "Congratulations, I remember this day so well. I am fine.

Love,

Calle."

I felt good last night for the war news was pretty good. Can't those Germans see the handwriting on the wall?

Well, this is the twenty-fifth page of this letter so I guess I will close for now. I hope you will be happy reading this let-

ter someday. I console myself with many happy memories of you, Dossi, and Karen. I have bought many cards for all occasions and none under fifty cents. I am trying to find a special card for you, but I have not found the right one yet. Take care and I hope we will be together soon. Good night and a thousand kisses I send to you today.

Your loving Calle

This was the last letter we have from Dad, written in 1943.

7
A FLOATING CATASTROPHE

April 20, 1944 was Hitler's birthday, and when a special party was organized in Bergen in honor of the Fürher, a number of high-ranking German officers came into town for the celebration. Meanwhile, amid all of the preliminary activities saluting the German dictator, something strange, unexpected, and diabolical was underway to add a special touch to the festivities.

An old steamship freighter from Holland called the *Voorbode* had been taken over and restored by the Germans. It was overhauled in Oslo, Norway in 1943. In 1944, it set sail for Kirkenes, in the northern part of Norway, bordering on Russia. In Oslo, it had taken on half its cargo, which happened to be dynamite, fuses, and caps.

One theory surrounding the presence of the explosives-laden *Voorbode* was that the Germans planned to keep it in the harbor at Kirkenes so that if they were forced to leave in a hurry, they could blow up the town and get away, leaving nothing but rubble behind.

The trip along the coast to Kirkenes included many stops, almost all under the cover of darkness. On one of the stops, more dynamite and fuses were loaded onto the ship. In the end, 100 tons of dynamite, 50 cases of fuses, and 180,000 caps were on board. On Sunday night, April 16, just three days before the planned celebration honoring Hitler, the *Voorbode* arrived in Bergen.

By law, explosives being transported were required to be divided into separate cargo holds, but the dynamite on this ship was all packed together in one storage compartment. The captain was instructed by the Germans to say only that bags of cement were on board.

The law also specified that a vessel with more than fifty tons of dynamite would not be allowed to operate close to shore. However, the Germans ignored all rules and regulations and told people that the *Voorbode* was just a routine supply ship bringing support materials to Norway. To all outward appearances, the vessel was simply in port for service and repairs and would leave the harbor when the work was completed.

But during its stay in Bergen, something went terribly wrong. Workmen had been making repairs to the *Voorbode* when a fire started on the ship. Within seconds, it reached the explosives and the ship exploded into a trillion fragments, causing the ground to shudder for many kilometers around.

More than one hundred Norwegians were killed by the blast and over five thousand suffered injuries. Buildings collapsed from the shock waves caused by the explosion, and destruction was everywhere. Famous landmarks like Håkon's Hall and Rosenkrantz Tower were heavily damaged. Flood water caused by the explosion lifted a two-hundred-ton barge from Holland out of the water and tossed it in the air like a toy.

Many thousands of people were affected by the explosion, some of them miles from where it had occurred, with shards of glass becoming imbedded into their skin and eyes. Unfortunately, there is no documented information about injuries suffered by the German officers who were commemorating Hitler's birthday.

After the explosion, the largest catastrophe in Norwegian history, sabotage was the first thought on everyone's minds. Though further investigation indicated that a fire in the coal bin had triggered the disaster, the Germans looked everywhere for scapegoats. Two men from Bergen who worked for the Norwegian Underground,* Rolfe Olsen and Trygve Havnes, turned out to be targets. They ran and hid but were found. In an attempt to capture them, one German soldier was killed but Rolfe and Trygve escaped.

No newspaper was printed in Bergen on this historic day, April 20. The Germans had stopped the presses so the explosion would not be featured in the paper. The next day, the headline in Bergens Tidende read, "Sorgens Slagskygge Over Bergen," which means "Sorrow Shadows Over Bergen."

Onkel Alf, who was married to Dad's sister Mathilde, worked for a company called Mowinckels which was located in an office building and warehouse directly across from the great ship explosion. Just before the explosion, Alf was looking out the window and noticed a fire on the ship. When he spotted the fire, he turned away from the window and walked toward the elevator. Within seconds the explosion occurred. At that very moment, the elevator door blew out and fell on top of one of his co-workers, killing him instantly. He was a young man who had recently been married. One other man was killed in the building, and many were injured.

Our cousin Arne Birkeland (his mother, Kristine, was another sister of Dad's) returned home after the explosion to find that the front door had been blown in against the steps by the impact and that the chimney had fallen to the ground in the rear of the house.

His mother and younger brother, John Henry, were nowhere to be found. They had gone to hide in the mountains in back of their home

* The Norwegian Underground, called Milorg, was organized in 1940 after the German invasion. Thousands of ordinary civilians took part in the movement, despite widespread fear that they would be punished severely if caught showing resistance to the Germans.

after the explosion, along with several other neighbors, not knowing if there would be any further explosions.

Mom, Karen, and I were all home at the time of the blast. I remember that the house shook and that we heard a loud bang. Because we were far enough away, our house was not damaged. But as we looked out our window, we could see the dark smoke over the harbor and it was obvious that something terrible must have happened. We didn't know immediately what had taken place, but the news soon reached us and over the next few days everywhere we went we learned of someone who had been injured by the explosion.

Many of the children living in Laksevåg and Bergen were sent to stay with farmers out in the country, away from the cities, during the summer of 1944. Bombings were increasing and food was scarce, and parents wanted their children out of harm's way.

The farm I was sent to was a dark, dreary place. and there were no children to play with. I was very unhappy there and decided to tell my mom in a letter how miserable I was. Soon, she had arranged for me to be returned to her.

Karen was luckier. She stayed with a nice family that included children her own age. She got along just fine with them and lived there for three months. The family wanted her to stay longer, but Mom missed her so much she brought her back home.

Though our parents were still unable to exchange letters at this time, Dad continued to write nearly every day expressing his feelings, worries, and thoughts on the war. It was not until the war in Norway ended in May of 1945 that he was finally able to mail all the letters and cards he had faithfully written over the years. He was also able to send all the gifts he had bought for our birthdays, holidays, and of course his and Mom's anniversaries. We were always on his mind, and he never forgot a special day. He was also very generous when it came to his Mom, Dad, brothers, and sisters.

Some of Dad's letters from 1944 show a remarkably good sense of humor; but behind the humor was serious concern for the well-being of his family in Norway.

July 29, 1944

My dear wife,

The war is still on, and I might as well keep writing. I have not written since last Sunday so now I am feeling lonesome. I am still fine and healthy, Madame Hoff. Hope you are the same. This war cannot last forever. Germany is in a fine fix now. They are being attacked from all sides. They have to give up one of these days . . . . That's all we can hope for. There are days when I wish that you could see me for I bet you would not believe that I am as close to heaven as I sometimes feel. These years have been terrible, but thoughts of seeing you again make me feel like I am in heaven. On the days I don't write to you I sit here and read your old letters or else I write cards to the girls. I sometimes write on the cards for them that I have already written on. They will probably tell you that their daddy sure messed up these cards, but when they see the money in them maybe they will forgive me. I will have to go to Pontiac and see if I can find some new cards. Well, I will stop for now and go and have a Dagwood sandwich before I go to bed.

Love to you all from Daddy.

August 2, 1944

My dear wife,

It is very hot now in Auburn Heights. I felt exhausted when I came home from work. We are now working from day to day to use up what we have already made. We are careful now not to make too much so we won't get stuck with a lot of weapons should the war end suddenly. I have not heard anything about Norway for a while now. I'm sure the Germans think the Americans and the Brits are the devil themselves.

Hope to see you soon.

August 5, 1944

My dear wife,

This is station L.O.V.E. broadcasting on a frequency of One Million Kisses. I hope my message comes through loud and clear. Is your receiving set working well, my dear?

Well, Madame Hoff, here I sit again. My thoughts of kisses for you are no fun on paper. Just think how wonderful it would be if we were in each other's arms, or in a rowboat on Puddefjorden. Maybe down lovers' lane where we could walk hand in hand and sing "Down through lovers' lane we will wander, sweetheart, you and I."

Soon we will be so happy, Olga. In the meantime we must be content knowing that we love each other so beautifully and completely. I can't help but write my feelings to you for you are in my dreams and thoughts and it helps to put it on

paper. Calle can never forget his life with Olga. So, Madame Hoff, keep your chin up and I will see you soon.

Love, Daddy

<u>*August 15, 1944*</u>

Another historic day in the course of the war. The Americans got in to the south of France last night, so now Hitler has more to worry about. The way it is going, we should have France in a few weeks. I have not heard much about the invasion but it was reported that we had a foothold on land there and that's all we need.

It is still warm, Olga, so everything is burning up. I woke up this morning and I thought I was freezing. I was lying on the bed naked with the windows open when a gust of wind woke me up. When I am writing to you, the heat is not so bad for I have you and me in mind.

<u>*August 22, 1944*</u>

My dear wife,

If I am not mistaken it was five years ago today that you and the girls left and sailed from New York. It seems impossible that we have been apart that long. What should I write today, dear? I think I have said just about all there is to say to the most wonderful woman in the world. My thoughts are with you and the girls all the time. The first thing I do when I get up in the morning is go to the window and look out, wondering what the three of you are doing. As the years go

by, I go around to some of the places where we had wonderful times. There are so many things I wonder about, especially how the girls look and feel.

Hoping you are all alive and well. I can't wait to have the girls call me "Far" in real Bergens talk. I will probably have many a good laugh the first few days, and will also be very proud. I sure hope that day comes soon.

I think of you always.

Daddy

<u>*August 27, 1944*</u>

Olga,

When I see kids and hear their voices, I especially think about our girls. Often I hear a song on the radio that starts me thinking about them. Some of the words are, "Somewhere, somehow, I find everyday reminders that are precious to recall." How can I think I have forgotten them, for forgetting is remembering after all. That's all for now.

Love to you all.

<u>*(later the same day)*</u>

I feel so alone right now I could cry. Nothing matters to me anymore, just you. I know I have to pull myself together, keep my chin up, and smile, but it is so hard. This war can't go on like this much longer. Sometimes I hear they are

pulling out of Norway, but then we hear so many things. I think I will go to a show.

Goodbye for now.

Calleman

August 29, 1944

My dear wife,

Yesterday I had one of those days where I was thinking about everything and did not feel like talking to anyone. I was surprised when one of the guys at work came up to me and asked me what was wrong, for they had not heard me sing all night. "Oh, I am just thinking," I said. For a few minutes I felt better. I keep hoping for a little message from you so I keep going to the mailbox, but I know there will be nothing there. In September, 1939, Hitler spoke about winning this war in five years, so maybe it will be over next month, but not with the results he expected. I went to Auburn Heights to look for mail again, but as I expected there was nothing. Take care.

Love,

Daddy

August 31, 1944

My dear wife, if it isn't the last day of the month! I warmed up the coffee and made a sandwich with ham and

tomato while I listened to hillbilly music. A little yodeling is good with your food. I listened to the radio this morning and it sounds good for our side. There won't be much left of Germany if Mr. Hitler insists on fighting to the last man. He has slowly begun to take his soldiers out of Norway. He has a lot of explaining to do to his homeland. We will have a celebration here the day Hitler falls.

The sky is blue again so I guess the rain is over. It has been very dry this year, just like the year we planted potatoes on Bessie Street.

Take care, my love.

Calleman

September 4, 1944

My dear wife, it is Labor Day today so summer is over in America. I am feeling good today, thanks to you as I finally got a message from you. It was sent April 15 so that was not too bad. I was so glad to hear that you were all alive and well. I was surprised to hear that Ingrid is getting married. I wish I could send her a few words for the occasion. The way things are going for the Germans, maybe they will be out of Norway by the end of the month. The way it looks here, everyone is expecting the Germans to give up any day. See you soon, my dear.

Love to you all.

Calleman

<u>September 7, 1944</u>

My dear wife and children, I have had a busy day today. There is money on the way to you, Olga, and a few words. I sent the money to Washington, D.C. I sent $400.00 and the way I understand it is, the money will be like a bank book for you. The most you can get is $80.00 a month but that should help a little. The bad part about this is there is no way I can let you know the money is underway. I am hoping that those who represent the U.S.A. in Norway will let you know about this bankbook. God knows I have tried to get money to you. I had just about given up hope that there would ever be a chance while the Germans were still in Norway. I was surprised when I finally got a letter from Washington saying that I would be allowed to send you money. This law was passed on May 25, 1944. I asked the Red Cross if they had known about this and they just found out a month ago. The only way I will know if you get the money will be if I get a notice from Washington. Maybe I will see you at Christmas. I feel good now that I am able to send you money.

Love,

Calleman.

<u>September 12, 1944</u>

My dear wife,

We are having an election this year so there is a lot of bullshit going on. The big boys from England and the U.S.

are meeting in Canada these days. They still have Japan to worry about, but I think they are pretty much done with Germany. The Allies are only three hundred miles from Berlin. It will be a race between the Russians, the English, and the Americans as to who gets to Berlin first. My spirits are up and down. Sometimes it is nice to feel a little romantically sad, the way you feel when you think about some lovely romantic experience that happened a long time ago, yet you feel a little sad when you can't relive that perfect moment over again. All I want to do is turn the clock back, the days, months, and years we have lost. That is how I felt this weekend. I felt so lost and helpless I wanted to cry, but I was grateful for the beautiful memories we have. Just sitting here, Olga, I fell in love with you all over again. You are more dear to me right now than you have ever been. No matter how brave I try to sound in my letters, I can't hide how much I miss you and love you. Say hello to Catherine and Karen. It has stopped raining.

Love,
Calle

<u>September 15, 1944</u>

My dear wife,

I have been sitting here looking out the window, thinking it is slowly starting to look like fall. The kids all registered for school today and will start on Monday. They normally

start right after Labor Day, but school was delayed this year because there has been such an outbreak of polio.

The handwriting is on the wall now for Mr. Hitler. The Americans have already taken several German cities. The folks there were scared of the Americans at first for they think of them as Indians! It was a while before the Europeans felt like they could trust the Americans, but when the GI's started handing out candy and cigarettes they all got smiles on their faces. There are so many things I want to tell you, Olga, and make you understand, but I am not always sure I go about it in the right way. I always want you to know how I am feeling and what I am thinking. I am always trying to picture in my mind's eye how you and the girls look while I sit here talking to you. My love for you and the kids is my whole life. The years of separation we have gone through become unbearable at times, but I try to keep my chin up and think about our future, when we will all be together again.

It won't be long now, Olga dear.

September 21, 1944

Hello, Madame Hoff,

Hope all is going well for you. Here in Auburn Heights all is the same. I am sitting here thinking about what you will need me to send to you when this war is over. I got a $100.00 bond yesterday so now my book is starting to look pretty

good. I now have $3,850.00 in bonds. It has taken your husband $3,000.00 to buy them and that is the most money we have ever had, Olga. I have not heard from Washington about the money I sent you. As soon as I know I will send more for I am sure you can use it. I only wish it did not take so long for you to get it. Boy, we are in a fine fix, Olga. You don't know what I am doing and I don't know what you are doing and there is nothing we can do about it. Everything will be okay in the end, I hope. In the meantime I sit here and worry and think about you.

I love you, my dear.

<u>September 26, 1944</u>

My dear wife,

I felt tough yesterday so I went to bed as soon as I got home. Guess I was all in for I slept ten hours. I was so surprised when I woke up and saw what time it was. I feel altogether different today. Well, Olga, let us talk about you a little. How are you and the girls doing? Do they mind you and are they good girls? When I finished writing you yesterday I sat and looked at pictures of the girls and read old cards that I had written to them over the years. Hope I will be able to send these things to you all for Christmas, but I doubt I will. I sure hope you get the money I sent you so you won't have to ask anyone for help. I don't know how things will be in Norway when this is all over, but I am sure it will be tough. If we are still at war with Japan after we finish with the Germans I doubt that I will come to Norway, so I

think it will be best if you come back here. What do you think, Olga? We have to be in agreement over that. Just so we keep our spirits up and stay healthy till then.

Love to you all.

Calle

8
A GERMAN BASE, A BRITISH TARGET, A SCHOOL DESTROYED

The German U-boat (submarine) base in Laksevåg was code-named "Bruno 1" and began to take shape in 1942, two years after Norway was invaded by the forces of Adolf Hitler. Construction was started after the Germans took control of the ship building yard in the northern bay of Puddefjorden as well as Laksevågsnes (the residential area) and part of the southern bay area.

The unfortunate people who lived on these sites were given just three weeks to move out; therefore, it wasn't long before the entire area was freed up for the Germans to take over. Families who had lived in these areas for generations were forced to spread out in different directions, some in Laksevåg and others in any available housing they could find.

When workers were needed to build the base, local residents were enticed to work for the Germans with the promise of good pay. However, working for the Germans was anything but a pleasure because workers were often treated in an abusive and demeaning way. After Germany attacked the Soviet Union in June of 1941, the Germans had unlimited access to Russian prisoners of war and used them as their labor force. The treatment of these prisoners was deplorable. Their clothes were rags and they wore makeshift shoes. Starved until their energy was drained then worked until they were exhausted, any prisoner caught eating out of a garbage can was shot on the spot.

Our house in Laksevåg was built on a mountainous cliff and the street in front to the house was about 25 feet below. In spite of the danger, many times Karen and I sat on the edge of the cliff and watched as several trucks filled with Russian prisoners of war drove past us. If we had any spare food, we would throw it into the open trucks as they drove by and the prisoners would catch the food and in turn would sometimes throw little wooden birds they had carved back to us. Once I caught a ring they had made out of scrap metal.

One day as I was walking to school, I passed a prisoner working alongside the road who put his hand out to me as if he were asking for food. I gave him the sandwich from my lunch bag but just then a German guard turned and noticed what I was doing. He grabbed the sandwich, threw it away, and motioned for me to go on my way. I was very lucky the guard didn't punish me for violating the rule.

In June of 1944, the Allied invasion of France had a tragic follow-up in Laksevåg that was tied to the German U-boat base. In the run of a few months, the Allied forces had conquered large portions of the French Atlantic seacoast. This meant that the Germans, who had their most important U-boat bases in Brest, Lorien, St. Nazaire, La Pallice, and Bordeaux, had to pull out and transfer their U-boats to German or Norwegian waters. Thus, in the fall of 1944, there was a noticeable increase in the number of U-boats in Laksevåg and the surrounding fjords.

When they built their base, the Germans had ignored the presence of Holen School, about 150 meters away. They claimed they had attempted to convince the local government to turn the school over to the Germans but that local authorities had refused to cooperate. This story was weak and probably false. A more plausible view is that they built the base there with the assumption that the Allies would not bomb the bunker with the school so close. Unfortunately, with the Laksevåg base in operation, the German fleet of submarines posed a serious threat to Allied convoys in the Atlantic and the North Sea. As a result, with its three dry docks and three in-water docks that could house as many as ten to twenty submarines in the base at any one time, Bruno 1 became the primary target of the British R.A.F. (Royal Air Force) bomber command.

As far as we know Mom had never before kept a secret from Dad. However, she never mentioned Bruno 1 in her hundreds of messages to him. There was a good reason for her omission: She knew he would worry himself sick about the safety of his daughters every waking moment. Since there was nothing he could do about it, she decided to do the worrying for both of them. But like many others in Laksevåg, she lived in constant apprehension that something disastrous was going to happen. She just didn't know what or when.

On October 4, 1944, the threat of danger became a day of terror. By the end of the day, 193 Norwegians had lost their lives, including sixty-one children at Holen School.

It started out as a beautiful fall day, with the weather calm and clear. As the morning unfolded, children were getting ready to go to school or were already in class. Businesses were beginning to hum and people looked forward to a typical autumn day. Everything seemed calm and quite normal.

Shortly after 9 a.m., an air raid siren sounded. My sister Karen was on her way to school and I had an appointment with the dentist. I was already in his office when the siren was heard. Mom immediately went after Karen and the two of them came and picked me up at the dentist's office and we ran for the bomb shelter.

We all knew this was the real thing, not just a practice drill, when we heard the hum of aircraft in the distance growing louder and more menacing by the second. Suddenly the clear blue sky became darkened by the presence of a fleet of bombers accompanied by artillery guns marking their arrival.

The air raid had begun in England early that morning with ninety-three Halifax and forty-seven Lancaster bomber aircraft. The air strike was being carried out by squadrons from the R.A.F., assisted by twelve Mosquitoes, very fast, lightweight British aircraft equipped with special radar that flew over targets and dropped markers to show bomber planes where to drop their bombs. Altogether, there were 152 planes with over a thousand troops on board on their way to bomb the German U-boat base in Laksevåg.

The Germans did not have any aircraft that could defend against the raid, but their anti-aircraft artillery fire was very effective, forcing the planes to fly at high altitudes. Trading for the higher altitude reduced accuracy in their bombings. In total, the planes dropped 1,260 bombs.

At Holen School, everyone had gone to the basement for protection after they heard the air raid sirens. However, the school was hit by several bombs that split the building in half all the way to the ground. In the woodworking hall, two entire classes died along with their teachers In the natural science hall, three classes of boys and one of girls suffered casualties. One girl died, the only female student to perish that day in the tragic bombing.

Rescue teams that came into the building after the bombing said that at the moment of impact, some of the children had clung to their teachers and were now almost impossible to separate.

In the bomb shelter we stayed close to Mom, more terrified than we had ever been before. A posted instructional card read as follows:

Sit still and keep spirits up.
Use small clear bright lamp (flashlight).
Do not use oil lamps.
Smoking is forbidden.
Do not leave shelter until person in charge gives OK.

During the air raid, a man came running into the shelter with his clothes on fire and men near the entrance tamped out the flames with their own clothing. He was burned and in shock and was shouting that the bombs had destroyed his house.

The attack lasted exactly eleven minutes from start to finish, but we remained in the shelter for a much longer period of time, waiting for the "All Clear" signal. When we went outside, the scene was unbelievable. Fires were everywhere we looked. Gas mains had been ruptured and the escaping gas fueled the fires. Roads were blocked by rubble and debris and water was pouring from broken pipes. The smell of gas hung in the air like a cloud that had been spread over the city by the bombers. Power lines were down and severed wires sparked wildly. Broken glass shone everywhere. A mask of shock, disbelief, and despair covered everyone's face. Parents ran to the school to look for their children and, for many, the news was devastating.

We were lucky. A bomb had landed directly behind our home, causing a huge crater in the ground and propelling pieces of shrapnel into the balcony of our building, but that was the extent of the damage we had to deal with. Many other buildings in town suffered major damage. Though the primary target of the air raid was, of course, the U-boat base, only minor damage was inflicted on the bunkers. Solidly built with reinforced concrete roofs about six meters thick with walls that were two to four meters thick, they had been designed to withstand the impact of the bombing.

Outside the bunkers, it was a different story. The entire area surrounding the school and base had been destroyed. The cleanup began almost immediately and lasted a very long time. Buildings had to be reconstructed or shored up, utilities had to be reconnected, and many people were homeless. Then the bombers returned two weeks later and bombarded the base once again.

In Laksevåg, there were no classes for months. Many of the utility power lines remained inoperative, road repairs were slow in coming, and local residents had difficulties even getting to their jobs.

But just days after the bombing, submarines were moving in and out of the U-boat base as though nothing had happened. To the surviving residents of Laksevåg, the devastating reality became obvious: Many lives had been lost; many lives had been wasted.

Immediately after the bombing, we left the city and moved to Vangsnes, in Sogn, where we would be safe from the war. We were scared, but very grateful to be alive. A friend of Mom's, Mrs. Teigland, was the one who was able to make these arrangements for us. We were all together on a farm and stayed there for seven months. Karen and I were also able to go to school in Vangsnes. We returned to Laksevåg in May of 1945 when the war was over.

The tragic results of the bombing, one of Norway's worst tragedies of the war, were as follows:

- 193 Norwegians were killed, including 61 students, 16 members of the Civil Air Patrol, 2 teachers, and a watchman.
- At Kleivdal's Leather Works, 36 died.
- At Iversen's Bucket Factory, 11 died.
- At the U-boat base, 12 Norwegian workers died.
- 54 people died in their homes or surrounding areas.
- 600 people were without homes.
- 40 homes were totally destroyed.
- 20 homes were damaged so badly they had to be torn down.
- A large number of Russian prisoners who had been working at the base also perished, though the Germans would not provide reliable information about this group of victims.

9
CONFLICTS CLOSE TO HOME

While the war was raging in Europe and our parents were living separate lives, writing letter after letter in a futile attempt to stay in touch and to relieve their loneliness, other family members in Norway were experiencing their own challenges related to the German occupation. No one was involved with the Germans more often than Magnus, one of Dad's younger brothers.

Onkel Magnus was a heavy smoker and didn't like being deprived of cigarettes during the war. One evening he was following a group of German soldiers who were smoking continuously and discarding their cigarette butts as they walked along the street. He picked up every used, smoldering, discarded butt he saw and carefully collected them in his coat pocket.

Showing no respect for Onkel Magnus and his recycling efforts, one of the soldiers threw his cigarette butt down on the ground and then stepped on it to crush it out. Magnus became so incensed by his condescending attitude that he lost his temper and punched the soldier in the face.

That act almost cost him his life.

In retaliation, the young man fired his gun wildly into the road. One of the bullets ricocheted and struck Onkel Magnus in the derriere while he was running away as fast as he could. His sister Borghild's apartment was nearby, so he took refuge with her for solace and repairs to his buttocks.

Onkel Magnus placed himself in danger in other ways, too.

During wartime, having a radio was forbidden by the Germans in Norway. But Magnus had one and cleverly hid it so it could not be found by the military. If it had, he would have been shot or imprisoned.

Just before the conclusion of the war, he placed his radio in the window of his apartment and turned up the volume so that everyone would know he had defied the German authorities and was now flaunting his transgression.

Another story told about Onkel Magnus involved German soldiers once again. Magnus and his wife, Borgny, were walking home one evening when two soldiers began to flirt with her, pushing her up against a wall.

Onkel Magnus was furious. He fought with both soldiers and threw them down a flight of stairs to the next street and then ran for cover with Tante Borgny. After the soldiers recovered from the rough treatment they had received from Magnus, they looked for the couple but never came close to finding them.

Finally, Onkel Magnus and Tante Borgny attended a party in Dolviken at Magnus' sister Anna's home. Unfortunately, they missed the last bus to take them home. Magnus devised a scheme to solve the problem. He simply scaled a fence, stole a bus, drove it home, and parked it outside their apartment. Then, with a muffled voice, he called the Transport office and told them where they could find their missing bus.

No one but his closest relatives knew that Magnus had taken the vehicle. Transport officials were baffled as they attempted to determine how it had arrived there. Was it stolen? By whom? For what reason?

Magnus may have taken a big risk, but no one ever suspected that he was the phantom driver, and he was never found out.

Other family members also had their trials with the Germans. In 1943, Dad's youngest brother, Einar (who at the age of 83 is the only surviving sibling of the Hoff clan), and his wife, Walborg, rented a room in their apartment to a young Norwegian woman. After she had been there for a few months, she was observed keeping company with a German soldier, behavior which was frowned upon by the locals. Onkel Einar and Tante Walborg couldn't tolerate this transgression and immediately asked her to find another place to live.

One evening as Tante Walborg was watching from the window in her apartment, she saw the woman approaching with her boyfriend. She knew right away that Einar was probably going to get involved and she begged him to leave because she feared for his life.

The couple came into the apartment building and demanded to know the whereabouts of Einar. When Walborg told the soldier that she didn't know where he was, the military man became angry and started to threaten the family. He fired a bullet into a wall to scare them and the round went through the wall and whistled over a bed with one of their children in it, narrowly missing the child. Another bullet damaged a lamp.

In the midst of all this confusion,Tante Walborg was able to phone the German military police to report the shooting and threats they were being subjected to.

For some unexplained reason, the soldier stayed while they waited for the military police to show up. He continued to scare the family by pointing the gun at Tante Walborg. In a gesture of bravery, she reached for the gun and took it out of his hand and threw it behind a cabinet.

Just then the German military police came, asked where the gun was, arrested the soldier, and pushed him down the steps. Tante Walborg shook for days after this incident.

Two members of our family worked for the Germans at the Laksevåg U-Boat base. Alfred Birkeland (who was married to Dad's sister, Kristine) was one of them and his family tells this story about his experiences while working for the Germans:

When the Germans began to occupy Norway, imports were discontinued. A number of men who had worked in the grocery business or home supply stores lost their jobs and were unable to find alternative work. Therefore, they were forced to work for the Germans.

Alfred's first job was at the U-boat base in Bergen. However, the base there was eventually destroyed and he went to work at the base in Laksevåg. There the Germans trained him as a welder.

On October 4, 1944, the day the British tried to destroy the Laksevåg base, Onkel Alfred was working in the facility. During the raid, several bombs fell on the bunkers but they could not be penetrated like the vulnerable Holen School.

Alfred was in an area hit by several bombs and everyone ran to get inside one of the bunkers. Alfred survived the attack but other men all around him were killed.

After this experience, he was never the same again. He was in shock and close to a nervous breakdown and could not bring himself to return to work at the base. Fearful that he could be forced to return, he went into hiding at the country home of Mathias Hoff (our Grandfather) until the end of the war.

Alfred tried to quit working for the Germans once before but had relented when the Germans had come to his home and threatened his family. His young son, John Henry, had been home at the time and the Germans had actually pointed a gun at his head during their threatening discussion with Alfred. They had held the gun close to John Henry and said they would pull the trigger if Alfred refused to return. He returned.

Our mom's brother, Johan Olsen, was also forced to work for the Germans during the war and he wrote about his experiences to Dad in a letter dated October, 1945:

Dear Carl,

I thought I would write a few words to you to let you know that we are still alive and doing pretty well. However, there were many times when the picture was dark and gloomy.

In the fall of 1941, fifteen or more of us were laid off from our jobs at the Hansa Brewery. There was no other work available so I had no choice but to go through the workers' office and they subsequently assigned me to the Germans.

I had a good job. I looked after four large electric compressors to make sure they worked properly. I worked with a Russian prisoner of war and he did all the unskilled labor.

I gave him food on several different occasions, but I had to be very careful. If the Germans had seen me giving him food, they would have sent me to Espeland (a concentration camp in Fana, Norway) or to Germany.

From the moment I started there, we were always in fear of an air attack. The first one came on October 4, 1944, killing many on the U-boat base and surrounding area. One of the bombs hit Holen School and 61 children died.

There was another air attack on October 29, and that came at night while I was working. At 1:10 a.m., the electrician came in and said that they were starting to bomb Gravdal and we should take cover. I couldn't hear what was going on when all the compressors were in operation, so I sent someone outside to see and listen and to let me know when the bombings were getting close to us so that we could take cover.

We had planned on going outside the U-boat base for cover, but once we stepped outside the door the planes were directly overhead. We had to run back inside where it was total darkness. The attack lasted an hour and a half and it was the worst thing I have ever gone through in my life. They came to bomb the U-boat base and there we were in the middle of everything. If they had used bigger bombs and the roof had not been so thick, we would all have been killed. We were lucky the roof held up. We had about fourteen or fifteen hits on the roof and they used time exposure bombs so it was dangerous to go outside even after the attack was over. We stayed in the U-boat base all night until morning. I wanted to go to the compressor house after my clothes, but this section had received a direct hit and was almost blown away so we were glad that we had survived.

After this incident, I was not able to go back to work. I was in shock so I stayed away from the base until January 9, 1945, but then a man came to my house and said that I had better return to work or be sent to Espeland or to a German camp. Then, on January 12, we had another attack and that was the worst of them all. I was on the night shift that week and this attack happened during the day so I was home. They used twelve one thousand-pound bombs and one bomb weighed six tons. The blast was so powerful that we felt it at Klosteret where I live. My wife and son were in the country with relatives so I was home alone. After this last incident, I left a note on my door saying I had hired on a fishing boat and that I was out to sea. They took the note and did nothing about it.

Well, Carl, I will stop for now and take this opportunity to congratulate you on your new freedom also and hope we will meet soon. Greetings from all of us to all of you.

Hilsen, Johan

In retrospect, we were very lucky we didn't experience at least one tragedy in those years. Many families we knew did lose family members as a result of the German occupation.

From the Photo Album

Dossi and Karen with their new spark, a gift from Bestefar Olsen.

Bestefar and Bestemor Hoff in front of home in Rådalen.

Karen and Dossi with Besemor and Bestefar.

Karen and Dossi looking out over the harbor.

Karen Hoff in the backyard of their house in Laksevåg.

Olga's sister Ingrid and the man she married in 1944, Anders Njøsen, a farmer in Sunnfjord.

Catherine (Dossi) and Karen show off outfits made by Mom.

Dossi, Karen, and friend Mossa in Laksevåg, Norway. Mossa is Dossi's best friend for life.

*Mom's brothers,
Sigurd and Johan Olsen.*

*Magnus and Einar Hoff,
dad's brothers.*

*Dad's sister Mathilde was
married to Alf Madsen.*

*Dad's sister Kristine was
married to Alfred Birkeland.*

Bergen: Destruction after explosion in harbor in April, 1944.

Aftermath of school bombing.

The Weather
Fair and cooler.
Details page two.

THE PONTIAC DAILY PRESS

HOME EDITION

[illegible]rd YEAR. * * * * PONTIAC, MICHIGAN, TUESDAY, MAY 8, 1945.

EUROPE'S WAR ENDS AT 6 P.M.; FEW NAZI UNITS FIGHTING ON

Doenitz Offers to Stay as New Reich Leader

Hitler's Successor Calls Upon German People to Work Hard as They Face Future

LONDON May 8 — (AP) — Grand Adm. Karl Doenitz, Germany's current fuehrer, announced today that all German arms would be silent by 11 p. m. (6 p. m., eastern war time) tonight.

Hitler's successor as fuehrer of the German people said in an address over the German controlled Flensburg radio that the Germans would lay down all their arms in accordance with the unconditional surrender terms he had ordered.

The German leader said that "German soldiers of countless battles now are treading the bitter path to captivity and thereby are making the last sacrifice for the life of our women and children and for the future of our nation."

"With the occupation of Germany," Doenitz said, "the power has been transferred to the occupying authorities. It is up to them to confirm me in my function and the government I have appointed, or decide whether to appoint a different one.

May Stay at His Post

"Should I be required to help our fatherland, I will remain at my post.

"Duty keeps me on my difficult post for the sake of Germany. I will not remain one hour more than can be reconciled with the dignity of the Reich."

Doenitz explained why he ordered surrender.

"When I took over from the fuehrer I took it as my first task to save the life of the German people.

"Therefore during the night of May 6 and 7 I gave the order for unconditional surrender. On May [illegible]

Okinawa Yanks Mile From Naha

Yanks Press on in East, Too Busy to Celebrate Victory in Europe

(By United Press)

Allied fighting forces in the Pacific pressed unremitting warfare against the Japanese today with no time out for celebrating the end of the war in Europe.

Military authorities predicted that, even with reinforcements from the European theatre, it would require another year to beat the Japanese on the mainland. They conceded, however, that Japan might surrender sooner.

The "war as usual" brought new Allied blows in the land campaigns on Okinawa, the Philippines and [illegible]

Prague Nazis Ignore Order, Looting City

Foe Troops in Norway Remain Inside Barracks Allies to Move In

BY ROMNEY WHEELER

LONDON, May 8. — (AP) —A handful of Nazi holdouts in Prague and some parts of the shrunken Moravia-Bohemia pocket fought on today as the rest of the world celebrated the end of the European war.

Czech broadcasts from the embattled capital said Nazis still were shooting, burning and looting in the city at noon in defiance of the signing of an unconditional surrender by their commander.

The patriots, now in control of all Prague [illegible], broadcast this noon report:

"Some German formations, disobeying the cease fire order, are shelling and setting fire to houses, shooting civilians and looting. Parts of Prague are in flames, and firemen are prevented by German gunfire from approaching the burning buildings. In some places in the center of the city German task formations are attacking Czecho-Slovak formations."

Yanks Nearing Prague

German broadcasts said that continued resistance in the southern pocket was designed to permit army remnants to retreat westward.

Gen. Patton's U. S. 3rd army had driven northeast from captured Pilsen to the outskirts of the capital and three Russian armies were driving toward the same goal from the east, northeast, north and southeast.

The patriot broadcast said Nazi Gen. Ferdinand von Schoerner, commander in Bohemia and Moravia, signed unconditional surrender [illegible] (battlefront time) [illegible] cease fire" [illegible]

One Yank's Thanksgiving Day

—AP Wirephoto

While New Yorkers stage wild celebrations of joy over Germany's surrender, S/Sgt. Arthur [illegible] of Buffalo, N. Y., who was wounded in Belgium, stands at the confetti littered corner of 42nd street and Lexington avenue watching the festivities, his own emotions surging with relief that at last its over in Europe.

Surrender Ratification Will Be Made in Berlin

Truman Proclaims End of Hostilities With Hitler but Says Job Is Not Yet Finished

LONDON, May 8. — (AP) — President Truman and Prime Minister Churchill today proclaimed complete victory in Europe. Hostilities formally cease at 6:01 p. m. E.W.T., tonight, supreme headquarters announced.

Shattered Germany's unconditional surrender "will be ratified and confirmed at Berlin" today, Churchill said.

Both leaders summoned their nations to a [illegible] the finish against Japan. Churchill reminded that "Japan, with all her treachery and greed, remains unsubdued," and Truman asserted that "when the last Japanese division has surrendered unconditionally, only then will our fighting job be done."

There was no immediate proclamation from Premier-Marshal Stalin.

Supreme Allied headquarters in a special communique said "Allied expeditionary forces have been ordered to cease offensive operations, but will maintain their present position until the surrender becomes effective."

Germany's unconditional capitulation to the western Allies and Russia was signed at 2:41 a. m. French time Monday (8:41 p. m., E.W.T., Sunday) this communique announced.

Supreme headquarters announced the Germans agreed to:

Order all resistance halted;

Yield all ships and aircraft unscuttled and undamaged;

Ensure compliance with all further orders from the Allied supreme commander and the Soviet high command.

The surrender document specified that nothing it contained limited or restricted any terms which might later be imposed upon the Reich.

TRUMAN PROCLAIMS END IN EUROPE

WASHINGTON, May 8.—(AP)—President Truman proclaimed today "complete and final" victory in the European theatre of the greatest war in history.

He went on a radio hookup at 9 a. m. (eastern war time) to read his formal proclamation, which he prefaced with brief remarks in which he solemnly warned:

"Our victory is [illegible]

[illegible]tiac Receives V-E Day [illegible]ence Quiet

Late War Bulletins

Allied Envoy Fly to Norway

NEW YORK, May 8.—(AP)—The British radio informed the German high command [illegible]

THE PONTIAC DAILY PRESS (Now *The Oakland Press*) May 8, 1945

Part 3

At Long Last, An End and A Beginning (1945)

On the afternoon of May 7, 1945, loudspeakers all over town confirmed Norway's freedom as the war with Germany came to an end. Everyone was in a festive mood. Children marched through the streets with flags and sang songs and shouted.

The first few days after the freedom was confirmed, people gathered throughout Bergen to celebrate with their friends and neighbors. In front of Bergen's largest department store, Sundt's, a large picture of King Håkon was displayed. Euphoria was the predominant emotion after so many years of misery. Bergen celebrated the freedom with a great display of lights, and the first free newspaper in five years went on sale. Headlines proclaimed the end of the war and the beginning of peace.

Like all Norwegians, we were happy that the sacrifices we had made for so many years were a part of our past. In recent years, food stations operated by Sweden and Denmark fed children, the elderly, and people who had been ill. Others stayed alive with whatever they were able to buy. During the war, for example, one small loaf of bread had to last one week, and margarine was made out of fish oil. Most adults did not have milk for three years but now began receiving one-half liter per day. Many Norwegians starved to death in those years, as the Germans took most of the available food and animals for their own use. Likewise, they did not allow fishermen to have fuel so they were unable to even take their boats out to fish.

With the once proud and aggressive German soldiers now prisoners of the Norwegian army, stories began coming to light of bodies of Norwegians found in the woods, murdered by Germans. Trials began for the many Germans and even some Norwegians who were charged with cruelty to the Norwegian people. When the figures finally came in, they showed that a total of 10,262

Norwegians had been killed, including seamen, political prisoners, members of the Norwegian underground, regular civilians, and Norwegian Jews.

The persecution of Norwegian Jews had begun in May of 1940, and in the winter of 1941-1942, Jews began to be arrested in large groups. Of the 769 Jews deported to Germany, only 25 survived. About half of the 1,800 Jews who lived in Norway when the war began sought refuge in Sweden, along with many other Norwegians. In fact, by the war's end, of the 92,000 Norwegians living abroad, 46,000 of them were in Sweden.

Dad's brother Einar, who was called into the military, was placed in charge of some of the German soldiers. His mission was to make the Germans point out and find mines planted around the city and the mountains. The Germans were then gathered up along with their belongings and marched out of town to be transported to prisoner-of-war camps. They were made to carry their belongings until they couldn't hang on to everything and dropped their possessions by the side of the road. Kids would then go through their things and take what they wanted.

Women who had befriended German soldiers were hunted down and had their heads shaved to mark them as traitors. Karen and I didn't participate in this but were bystanders watching the older boys do it until the practice was finally stopped by the police. By that time, the women were marked and had to wear scarves around their heads.

More than half a century later, I can still feel the excitement that came with the announcement that the war was finally reaching an end and that the combat, bombings, and other terrible aspects of war were concluding. With parties and freedom parades going on all over town, it was a happy time to be free at last.

10
DREAMS BECOME REALITY

In the excitement that overwhelmed them immediately after the war, Mom and Dad began to make plans for the reuniting of their family. The decision to move back to Michigan was made by Dad, and Mom concurred confidently. The war had cost them six years of togetherness. Now they were ready to become a family once again.

Some of the letters they wrote immediately following the conclusion of the war captured the wonderful feelings of relief and optimism we all felt. Their letters also brought to light just how out of touch they'd been for so long.

June 4, 1945

My darling Calle,

How are you? We are finally able to write to each other again and hopefully we will be back together soon. It is wonderful to be free again, almost unbelievable. It's like waking from a bad dream. Now we can sit and talk freely and do what we want. It has been six long, dark years, but luckily no one in our family died or was put into prison.

For the past seven months, the girls and I have been living in Sogn. I wrote several Red Cross letters from there which I hope you got.

Last fall, it was pretty bad in Laksevåg. Germans were everywhere, so there was no peace day or night. We were lucky to get a place to stay in Sogn. We got good food there and the girls changed a lot, especially Karen. She was so depressed and nervous from all the bombings.

We came home from Sogn a week ago. All three of us are fine. Last week I got your telegram and we were so happy to hear from you at last.

In town, people are fighting over what little food there is. We are not starving exactly, but we do not have much to eat. Food is starting to come into the country now and thank God for that. We are longing for something good to eat. Tomorrow is Dossi's thirteenth birthday. She's a big girl for her age and so is Karen. In your telegram you asked me what we need. The girls need everything, especially dresses, so please send whatever you can. Dossi only has wooden shoes. It's been two years since we have been able to buy shoes. Schooling has been very poor these last few years so the girls have a lot of catching up to do. We have good girls, Calle, and they will bring us much happiness in the future.

June 7, 1945

Dear Far,

Now it has been a long time since I have seen you, but I think I will remember you. You must come home to us now. There are many whose fathers have come home these days and some whose fathers have died. I am supposed to start the fourth grade, but we have no school and my teacher has died. My friend also died with her Dad and Mom at their house. Many others that we know also have died, but we are alive. Mor said that you would be sending me something nice when you can.

Take care, Far.

Karen Marie

July 1, 1945

Dear Calle,

We are fine here now, but I'm very anxious to get a letter from you to hear how things have gone with you these past years.

Do you think we should return to the U.S., or will you come to Norway?

We are still not able to get any clothes, and it is true what you have read in America that we have paper shoes and clothes and hand towels. I have paper curtains in one of our rooms.

When you have a chance to send the children some clothes, crease or crumple them together or wash them first and send them as used clothing. Otherwise, the duty we have to pay is so very high.

This week we are getting some good English Sunlight soap and we are really looking forward to it. We haven't been able to get good soap for years; as a result, the girls' hair has gotten so dark and gloomy looking because I haven't had any good soap.

Have you changed much in your appearance, Carl?

Goodbye for now. I miss you so much.

July 8, 1945

Dear Calle,

Many women here have their husbands back from the war at sea. Food supplies are improving and it appears the shortages are over.

Karen has been going with her friends on trips to Sydnes for swimming and has become a good swimmer. She is always active, never still. On Sundays she is up first and makes coffee and sets the table so everything is ready for breakfast when I get up. Dossi is quite different, with a quiet temperament. She enjoys reading and follows my instructions closely. They are both good girls, Carl.

Remember that tooth Dossi broke a few years ago? Well, now she needs to have additional work done to repair what has worn out. As a result, she has been to the dentist several times.

July 14, 1945

Today I got five postcards from you. You ask if we need money, Calle, but I thought you were paying for the 343 kroner I get through the government every month. I get it through the Norwegian Credit Bank in Oslo and have been receiving it since last August.

You did not say if you are coming here or if we are coming to America. I will wait to hear what your plans are for the future. I'm just glad we are all alive and well and we can write to each other.

I miss you.

Love,

Olga

July 25, 1945

I was so happy when we came home for in my mail box we had twenty-nine postal cards from you and two air mail letters. The girls and I were so excited, we didn't know where to start.

I don't have your letters to myself any more, because Dossi reads them as fast as I do. Karen isn't able to read your handwriting, so she says her dad should write plainer so she can read them.

The American Consulate in Oslo has notified us that the money they were sending each month has stopped, since it was only made available during the Germans' occupation of Norway.

My dad is in the hospital with a type of tuberculosis affecting his lungs. The doctor said the type of TB he has is not contagious. I'm so glad he can stay in the hospital because there he gets food and it is nice and warm.

He is hoping to come back home from the hospital in a few months.

July 29, 1945

We are in Sunnfjord now, visiting Ingrid and Anders. They have a small house for themselves; however, there are many brothers and sisters who also live on the farm.

Anders also has a workshop near here where he makes furniture. It is hard to picture Ingrid living in the country and married to a farmer. She never dreamed, when she returned to Norway six years ago, that she would settle on a farm in Sunnfjord for the rest of her life.

Last week, Crown Prince Olav visited Bergen and Laksevåg and I'm sorry we were unable to see him, but we heard his talk on the radio from Laksevåg. He said that Laksevåg was the hardest hit town in Norway during the war, except for the very northern area. He also mentioned the tragedy at Holen School.

There is much unemployment in Norway these days, and I heard on the radio that there is a lot of unemployment in the U.S. as well.

What have you decided about our future? It would be a good idea for you to take a trip to Norway for your parents' sake. Do you think we should stay in Norway? What do you think is best for us to do?

August 15, 1945

We are now home in Laksevåg. This day has been full of surprises. I called the post office as soon as I got home and asked if there was any mail for me. The postman just laughed and said to bring a big suitcase and a wagon for there was that much mail from America for us. He said there was too much to deliver and that I would have to pick it up.

Dossi and I went to town to pick it up and when he brought it out we could not believe our eyes. He had seventy-five cards and sixty-nine letters for us and then all the packages and magazines. There were many envelopes addressed to the girls and they were so excited each time they opened one, for in them there were hair pins, ribbons, and pictures. Tonight, the girls had all their friends over to see all the stuff they had gotten. They were all so excited, laughing and talking, Calle, you should have seen them.

They have not had much to get excited about these last few years, so they want to write to you right away. Karen put her yellow hair ribbon on and Dossi put the two small red ones on. She still parts her hair in the middle. I have been sitting for two hours, reading some of your letters. I have a little lamp by my bed, so I will read more tonight when I go to bed. Remember how I used to sit in the window and watch for you to come home and how happy I felt when I finally saw you? I often dream about being in your arms, talking about what we have been through in the past six years. The beautiful nightgown you sent I will save for our "wedding night."

Now the war is over and we will be together soon and we have two wonderful girls to be happy about. When we came home from Sunnfjord the bells were ringing and Bergen was all decorated with flags and banners. It is starting to get dark early now, but this winter will be much better for now we have street lights on again.

I had a wonderful time showing Sigurd and Ingeborg all the things you sent to us. We had sandwiches and the cocoa you sent. A thousand thanks for everything.

Love,

Olga

August 17, 1945

Our Dear Son Karl,

Many thanks for the dear thoughts your mother and I have gotten from you today. One of the letters is dated July and one from June and the other from May 1945. We are very happy to get these letters from you. We sent you a letter a short time ago which we hope you have gotten. I will try to tell you a little about how things are for us now after the years of hardships we have suffered through. Things are a little better with food now, but clothes and shoes are impossible to buy. I have some, but your mother's clothes are all worn out, but we hope things will be better soon. Many mornings when we awoke all we had to eat was one bread end. There were times when we did not have anything to eat, so I don't understand how we all lived through it. There were many people here who starved to death. Your brothers and your sisters here are all fine.

Your brother Einar is in the military. He has been assigned to stand guard over the Germans, but soon they will be out of the country. Otherwise with us, we have worked hard in our time and now time is taking its toll on us. As you know, Karl, your mother and I have had long working days behind us and are now starting to be very tired. It has not always been easy for us raising a big family, but we have had so much happiness from our children. I can't tell you in one letter, Karl, about all the murders and and cruelties they have done in our country. Many bodies of Norwegians have been found in the woods that the Germans murdered. There are many Germans and some Norwegians who will stand trial for their many cruelties to the Norwegian people. I hope you will come home soon, Karl. We won't be short of stories to tell.

I hope you will come home for our big day November 19th, our 50th wedding anniversary. I want to thank you so much for all the packages and dear thoughts to your mother and me as well as all your brothers and sisters. I am sure there is not another son that thinks more about his family than you do. With these words I will end with a greeting from my heart from all of us.

Mom, Dad, and Family

August 19, 1945

Calle,

I both laugh and cry in the evening when I'm reading your letters. I often go to bed with a few letters and read until two or three in the morning.

I'm very happy now, but I am also anxious to know what our future will hold. We will need to talk about our plans, and that makes me even more anxious to have you back with us.

The weather in Norway is so great this summer, with sunshine every day, and it would be wonderful if you were here. Karen has been swimming every day in Sydnes or other places. She knows her way around here now. Unfortunately, Dossi has not been able to swim much because she doesn't have a bathing suit, but she borrowed Ingrid's bathing suit and brought it home.

Karen doesn't seem to gain weight no matter how much I feed her, but Dossi has put on a few pounds. However, Karen looks much better now than when she left to live on the farm in Oslofjord. The winter before she was very thin and did not look good and I was ready to cry because I didn't have anything good for the children to eat. For example, they ate some dry bread before they went to school without milk, because we didn't have any. Once they were in school,they got some oatmeal. The small portion of milk given each child they drank in the afternoon, so they had none for breakfast or in the evening. Thank goodness those times are over.

Yesterday, we were able to get many good things at the store. We actually got eggs, which we haven't had for five years. It doesn't seem possible that many kids under five have never seen an egg. In the fall we are going to get bananas and oranges. We were also excited to get two kinds of cheese.

There is a lot of unemployment here now, but we hope it lasts for only a short time during the changeover from war to peace. The leaders of our country predict many good things for Norway. But, at the same time, we are very dependent on imports for building materials and other items.

As for our future, I keep thinking and thinking and I don't come up with a clear-cut answer. That's why we need to talk, Carl.

August 23, 1945

Dear Calle,

I have been reading and re-reading all of your dear letters and last night I finally came to the bottom of the stack we received when we came home from Sunnfjord.

Yesterday three new letters arrived, the last of which had a post-mark of August 8, so the mail is faster now but the letters are still being opened and censored.

Now that Japan has surrendered, the mail probably won't be opened any more.

What are you doing these days? Are you working?

The girls are so longing for you to come home. Your return is all they talk about these days — that and all the packages of good things you send them. I am so happy, I feel like a child again myself.

Thank you for the raincoats you sent us. They really needed them. It's just amazing that you are able to tell from such a distance what they need.

I tried for about eighteen months to get some material for coats for Dossi and me and I have finally gotten it. I've found a tailor to sew mine, but it will probably take a long time before it is done because the tailors are so busy now that everyone is able to buy material.

While I'm thinking about it, we need garters, stockings, and underwear . . . and, by the way, someone said to me recently that I look ten years younger than I did a couple of years ago.

I'll let you be the judge.

I read in the paper today that two hundred Norwegian prisoners had been released from a prison in Germany. Their families had given up hope of ever seeing them again, so you can imagine how happy they were. I was at the railroad station when some prisoners came home and it was so touching and sad to see their mothers, wives, and sweethearts welcome them back home and then to see how bad some of them looked. It made me cry, so I never went back. I have cried enough in the past few years, so now we must look forward to the future.

Love,

Olga

August 26, 1945

This is Sunday afternoon and I'm all alone. The girls are out with friends and will return around suppertime. I am very sad today because of the news I must share with you.

Carl, your dad passed away of a heart attack last Wednesday, August 22. It's too bad this had to happen now, when we are all so happy to have survived the war.

After returning home, he went after some water down the road because his own well was dry. When he got there, he didn't feel strong and decided to go back home. He went down to the basement and sat on a stool. Shortly after that, he called up to your mom in the kitchen and asked her to come down because he was suffering chest pains. But before she could get to him, he died.

Your mom didn't know what to do, but she called a young couple who were working in the field across from them and they came and helped get him upstairs into the house. Then they called the doctor and Borghild, who called all of your sisters and brothers and told them the sad news.

It is difficult to explain why your dad was taken from his loved ones at this time, but it's God's doing and only He can fully understand the situation. But you can take comfort in the fact that your dad received your letters before he died, because I watched him wipe tears from his eyes as he read them and comment that you were the best son anyone could have.

I am sorry, Carl, and I love you.

August 29, 1945

Dear Carl,

It has been many years now since I last wrote, but it was because of this terrible war that we have all been through. We are all happy here at home now to have our freedom, and now it is over between America and Japan too. With all this happiness over our freedom, we were all saddened by Far's death. We just got back from the funeral when I had this strong feeling to write to you. Far was buried from Molendale Chapel, and he wishes to be buried in Bergen. He had a beautiful service with many flowers and a wreath from all of you in America. It was red, white, and blue and laid down by pastor Gulbrandsen.

There were many people at the funeral, for Far was loved by everyone. Magnus laid down a wreath from all of us here. I hope you can come home soon, for Mor is thinking so much about you.

Love from your brother Einar.

September 3, 1945

We are all fine, Calleman, and enjoying all the wonderful things you are sending us. We have so much fun with Karen and her new blue morning robe. You should have seen her when she opened it, she was just beaming with excitement. Look, Mor, she said, it goes all the way to the floor, and we love the beautiful color. Thank you so much for everything, my darling, especially the soap. The girls love the cocoa you sent. I have to fix it in the morning and in the evening. I was looking over my meat card and the last time we had meat was in April of 1942. The Germans took so many animals from the farmers, there is nothing left to slaughter.

The girls started school today. Karen is going to the old Damsgård School and Dossi has to go way out to Nygårdsvik School. They have not been able to go a full school year these past years, for something always seems to happen. We lived in a pretty dangerous place all these years, but that is all over now.

Your dad's funeral was on Wednesday. He had a beautiful service. I have never seen so many beautiful flowers and so many people. The chapel was full, for your dad was loved by so many people. After the funeral we all went to Tilla's house. Your mom is going to live with Einar this winter. Borghild will also be living there with them. She will be of great comfort to your mom. I got a letter from my dad's doctor and he will not be coming home after all. They found that he still tested positive for tuberculosis. Take care, darling.

Your longing
Olga and girls

September 10, 1945

I'm waiting for a letter from you from New York. I have been worried about you and hope your trip went okay. I'm home alone now, since Karen is at a scout meeting and Dossi is out with a friend. The autumn weather is spectacular and I wish so much that you were with me. We all miss you desperately.

We still have a few Germans here in Laksevåg. This is where they are all sent before they are shipped out. You better believe we enjoy watching them march by the thousands with the Englishmen in control. It is not like when they came marching in during the invasion. They sure don't like to be ordered around. It is with a heavy heart that they leave Norway for they had it good here. They took all our food and let our poor children go without. If it had not been for the Danish, our kids would all have starved to death.

Yesterday we had mutton for dinner. We also were able to get Danish pork on Saturday, but all food is very expensive. I still have a little more than 1,000 kroner, so you don't have to send us any more money.

All the money in Norway is going to be confiscated and we will be issued new currency.

Oh, the children just came home and are asking for food, so I'll have to tend to them for now. They truly enjoyed the cocoa you sent and we'll finish the remainder of it tonight, so please send us a new supply if you can. The girls say hello to you, Calle.

Your loving

Olga

September 20, 1945

Dear Carl,

My dad is home from the hospital for a little while. He has to go back soon for there is something else wrong. Poor Dad, he looks so bad. He is going to a specialist tomorrow. It is not good to be old and sick. I have been so depressed this week for everything seems to have gone bad all of a sudden. Ingrid is coming home here to see Dad, for no telling how long he will live. We are all fine and enjoying your packages with all the wonderful things you are sending. It is hard to get food now again. It was pretty good right after the war ended, but now the store shelves are empty again. Take care, darling. I will write again soon.

Love,

Olga and girls

September 26, 1945

Ingrid came home on Monday to see Dad. He has to go back to the hospital soon. Dossi and I have been studying English tonight and she is pretty good. She has English in school and her teacher gets a good laugh out of her for she has such an American way of pronouncing her words. She is going to be very good by the time we come back to America. In your letter you wrote that you thought Karen looked thin. She is thin, Calle, but I have done everything I can to give her good food. It is just hard for her to gain weight. Children under twelve years old got a chocolate bar today, so Dossi did not get one. Will write soon again.

Love,

Olga and girls

October 1, 1945

Ingrid just returned home, so we are alone. We have things so cozy when we are here by ourselves. It is getting dark very early now so the girls are in bed early and they fall asleep by eight o'clock.

Dossi gets very tired from doing homework, which she starts after we eat. She sits and works at the homework for a few hours. The girls have missed so much school, they have a lot to make up. I'm glad that she is so interested in English and I'm also glad that I can help her with it. She will start school when we come back to America, so these English lessons she has now will be a big help.

We all had a very nice time with the Engelsens on Sunday. She had pork steak, vegetables, tomatoes, potatoes, and a good gravy. For dessert, a fruit pudding with cream. Ingrid and I and the children have talked about this dinner every day since we were there and we agree that it was one of the best meals we have had in Norway. Don't forget that we haven't been able to get pork steak in the last five years.

She had also baked a large round cake with jelly inside and cream on top plus cookies that we had with our coffee later in the afternoon. Then, you won't believe what happened. They insisted that we eat with them in the evening and you should have seen the table, Carl. It was full of delicious food once again. They haven't heard of rationing up there.

They are still running a pig farm, with about fifty large pigs and a few little ones. They have a lot of work taking care of so many animals, but they are making a lot of money with the farm. They own lots of property and are now going to sell part of it. Gustave said he wanted to take a trip to America, and will probably do it soon. He still hasn't married.

On Sunday, the Stavangerfjord *came from America with a lot of passengers. We didn't have a chance to go to the dock since we were away, but the ship received a great welcome from lots of people, with music and fireworks.*

There is lots of mail from the arrival of the Stavangerfjord *and they are sorting it at the post office. You have been so kind and considerate in what you have been sending to me and the girls, and we perk up every time the ship comes in.*

On Saturday, we will get pictures of Dossi. I hope they are good, because we didn't get to look at any proofs this time because of the paper shortage. I have a picture of Karen taken in 1943 that I will send you also.

You have sent me so much good reading material that I lie long into the night looking at and reading all the magazines. Small Homes *is a particularly interesting publication that makes me wish for a pretty little house with an electric stove and a bath with an electric water heater. This we must have in our new home. Can we get a house built and pay so much a month? That way you won't have to use your bonds.*

Furniture we can buy a little bit at a time as we can afford to do so. The girls are big and need their place, you know. It would be nice if you could find something for us so that we don't have to live with anyone.

I haven't gotten an answer from the Consulate in Oslo yet, but it should be here any day. The girls are looking forward now to traveling to America, they tell me, so we must begin to get ready.

There is a walking competition going on these days. It is called the "Freedom Walk" and if you can walk five thousand meters in forty-five minutes you get a pin to wear. It costs two kroners and the money will go toward the rebuilding. I made it in forty-two minutes and Karen came in first in her class. Dossi did good too. She had eight minutes to spare. The king was here in Laksevåg and Karen and her friend Unni gave him a bouquet of flowers. They went to the market in the morning and bought the flowers and were so proud to be able to give them to the king. I have more to write about, Calleman, but if I use another sheet I won't be able to send this letter by airmail.

Love from all of us for now.

Olga and girls

<u>*October 8, 1945*</u>

Got a letter from you today, Calle, and I feel so sorry for you. You are sending packages and struggling in your loneliness and trying to think of everyone. You have to stop sending us so many things since we will be coming to America as soon as we can.

I wrote to the Consulate in Oslo a while back and asked them when we would get our papers, but they have not answered me yet. I went to Bennet's Travel Agency on Saturday and he said I had to make a reservation now if I wanted to travel to America before Christmas because there are so many who want to come over, many seamen, business folk and ordinary passengers, and also American citizens. Now I don't know what to do since I haven't heard from the Consulate. I will have to wait for the time being.

Where are we going to live, Calle? It won't be so good for us or for Margit and Ted if we live with them. The Stavangerfjord *sails from here October 13 and it will return from New York on November 1.*

I am mailing this letter by airmail in the morning and then I will write an ordinary letter that will go on the Stavangerfjord *along with two pictures of the girls and some newspaper clippings and magazines. Karen wrote you a letter today and that will also go on Saturday. Dossi will write also, so you will get a lot of mail.*

We haven't gotten any packages since I wrote to you last, but all the mail hasn't come yet. There was an article in the newspaper that the Stavangerfjord *could not take all the mail that was going to Norway. They had so many packages that several thousand were left in New York. Today we got a dispatch note about a package from Tante Olga to Ingrid. On the note it says it is used clothing. I will pick it up tomorrow and send it to Bygstad.*

On Saturday I received a dispatch note for your mother from Margit. Magnus came over with some potatoes for us so I gave him the note about the package because your mother lives with him now. Magnus was very happy with the suit you sent him. It was a perfect fit.

I am sure that everything you have sent us has reached us now and I have made a note of the packages we have received and I will mail that to you on Saturday.

I think I will end this letter now and write to you again tomorrow. I will send it on Saturday. We are all well here. Karen was so happy that she had written you a letter. I think she had a guilty conscience since she hadn't written to you for a while.

Loving greetings from your wife and children

October 10, 1945

I went to the shipping office today to find out about tickets to America. There are two ships leaving before Christmas. It won't be a problem for us to get tickets as long as we have our visas. I still have not heard from Oslo so if I don't hear today I will write to them again. What do you think, Calle? When should we come? The tickets are quite expensive. For third class it is $200.00 per person and for tourist class it is $260.00. Third class is fine and then we will save a lot of money. I will wait to hear from you. I miss you so much.

Karen is finally starting to look better. I had her see Dr. Westergard and he said she is fine except she is anemic. She has to take iron pills and cod liver oil. We go back to the doctor next week. Ingrid has sent us some good butter from the country and that makes everything taste so much better.

We have come a long way these past few months. It is so good to have peace again and now we can get undressed and go to bed and sleep without having to worry about bombings. Before, we always left some of our clothes on and only halfway slept, just waiting for the sirens to go off, and that played on our nerves.

Our girls are sure different, Calle. Dossi is very quiet and likes to sit and read when she is done with her homework. I have to make her go outside once in a while for she needs the fresh air. Karen, on the other hand, is always on the go. She runs out as soon as she has swallowed her food. I hope all is well with you, Calleman.

Love,

Olga

October 19, 1945

Well, Calleman,

We will soon be together again. I think we will leave on the ship that sails in November if we can get everything in order by then. I wrote directly to Oslo so I am sure we will hear soon. Karen's coat came and she was so excited she sang, laughed, and danced around like she was not all there. You should have seen her. She looks so cute in red. It was just as if you saw Sonja Henie in one of her fur coats, that's how pretty she looked. The next day your package came with all the cereal and other things. Karen loved the box of All Bran. She thought it was the best thing she had ever had. It is almost gone already. I made a good evening meal and wanted to surprise the girls so I decorated the table real pretty and had all that good food out. The girls were surprised and said how pretty everything looked and how good everything tasted. Karen ate seven sandwiches and had three cups of cocoa. I felt like we needed to celebrate a little tonight since we had so many good things to eat. I am always happy when I can give the girls good food for there were so many times I cried for I did not have food to give them. Our cupboards were always empty.

Yesterday I took Karen back to the doctor and she is doing much better. She has taken one hundred of her iron pills and has a hundred more to go. She now weighs thirty kilograms. Your mom is knitting your sweater and hopes to have it ready by the time we leave.

Two weeks from today is our anniversary, Calle, so I will say Happy Anniversary now. I don't have any film, Calle, so I can't take a picture of the girls in their new coats, but you will see them soon. Thanks a million for all the wonderful things we got this week. I will try to get everything ready so we can leave on the ship that leaves November 19. I sure want us all to be together for Christmas. I will send you a telegram to let you know.

Love from all of us.

Olga.

October 20, 1945

My darling Calle,

These two girls of ours are the luckiest little girls to have a daddy like you. They look like two little rich girls in their new coats in comparison with what they had to wear before. Calle, I don't think I have told you lately how much I love you and how lucky I am to have you. I feel no sadness these days for we are finally going to be together soon. That will be the happiest day of my life, to have all four of us together again after all these years. What an outstanding man you have, Fru Hoff, people tell me when they see all the packages you send us, and my heart just swells up with pride. It has been very hard for all of us these last few years, but that is all over now. We are all so lucky. See you soon, Calleman.

Love,

Olga

October 23, 1945

I have been thinking so much about you today, Calleman. I am sure you were very surprised to get my telegram saying we will be on our way in less than a month. I have to go to Oslo to get my papers in order. Ingrid will come and stay with the girls, as she has to come here anyway to get some of our things that she wants to take back to Sunnfjord with her. There is so much to do before November 19. It is hard to believe, Calle, that we will soon see each other again. The girls are so anxious to see you, especially Karen, because she can't remember you. She is glad you are not bald. There won't be many more letters now, Calle, before we leave. Your mom is trying to get your sweater finished before we leave. All three of us are fine. Will write more later.

Love,

Olga

October 29, 1945

Believe me, Calle, I am trying to get things in order for our trip. There are so many papers we need. We have to show proof of citizenship, copies of our birth certificates, marriage certificate, and passport pictures. They told me I did not have to go to Oslo as they had already received the guarantee statement from the bank in America. As I am a Norwegian citizen, I had to show proof that my husband had money in the bank to take care of us. I also got a call from the hospital about my dad. It was from the head nurse and she told me my dad is not doing well. He had suddenly become very sick during the night and if I wanted to see him, I should take the first boat there, so I will go there the first thing in the morning. There is a slim chance that he will recover from this. I hope he will be all right. I am so looking forward to seeing you again. If all goes well, I will see you around November 30. It's almost unbelievable.

See you soon, Calle.

Your Olga, Dossi, and Karen

November 12, 1945

I did have to go to Oslo last week to get things in order with my visa and such. They could not get it ready while I was there so they will send it to me right away. I will tell you all about it when I see you. Today I bought our tickets so now we won't have many more days in Norway. The girls are very excited and have high hopes about what is ahead for them in America. I hope they won't be disappointed. We are going to have a wonderful Christmas, Calle, the four of us. My dad is not well. Ingeborg and I went to see him and he did not know us. He had a stroke. Ingrid is there now as she stayed with the girls when I went to Oslo. I am looking forward to this trip. I have so much to tell you.

Love from all of us.

Olga

This is the last letter we have that Mom wrote. Our grandfather died on November 19, 1945, the night we left Norway.

11
TOGETHER AT LAST

Five months had passed since the war ended in Norway when Mom and Dad finally made the decision that we would return to America and hopefully be together again before Christmas. Following that decision, there was a lot to be done before we could leave.

Tante Ingrid came in from Sunnfjord to help us prepare for the departure. While we were getting ready to leave for America, we visited with Bestefar Olsen in the hospital. He was very ill and Mom went to see him as often as she could, but he was getting weaker by the day. Onkels Sigurd and Johan would still be close by to look after Bestefar and let us know how he was doing after we left. Sadly, Bestefar Olsen passed away on November 19, 1945, the day of our scheduled departure. Now Mom had to be strong once again for us all, since there was nothing she could do for Bestefar except to keep him in her heart.

Karen and I had made many friends during our stay in Norway and we shed a lot of tears as we said goodbye to them and to our family. Karen's fourth grade class gave her a silver spoon engraved with the message, "Erindring Fra 4 Kl. Bergen 1945," which means "a remembrance from the fourth grade class, Bergen 1945." I also received a silver spoon from Miss Nilssen and my classmates.

When Mom, Karen, and I sailed on November 19, 1945, we met rough seas once again, just as we had on previous trips. And, since we were on one of the first ships to venture across the ocean after the devastating war, our captain and crew had to maneuver around unexploded mines that had not yet been disarmed or destroyed. We wore life jackets on deck several times because of the inherent danger of the mines. We were all thankful that we did not encounter any problems along the way.

On the morning we arrived back in New York harbor, there was a large crowd of people on the dock awaiting the arrival of our ship.

Dad couldn't wait to get to the dock that day. In his attempts to get as close as possible to the gangplank, he found himself in a restricted area and had to be escorted by security guards back to where he was supposed to be — which was farther away than he wanted to be. He was obviously anxious to see Mom, to wind his arms around her, and to tell her how much he loved her. But he was also especially eager to see Karen and me, for he knew that we had changed so much in the six years since we sailed for Norway in 1939.

Mom was the first one to spot Dad in the surging crowd, and she pointed him out to us. We didn't recognize him at first because he was dressed in a large overcoat and a hat. He was happy to see us at long last, and we all cried and hugged each other. It was a tender, warm, wonderful moment for our family.

First dozens, then hundreds, then thousands of times, Mom and Dad had envisioned this special day while they were on separate continents, on opposite sides of the Atlantic Ocean. And as they came together for the first time in six years, they were both unsure of what they would say to each other. Many thoughts darted through their minds. Finally, here they were, face to face, hugging each other and filling each other's ears with words of love.

Dad felt bad when he saw us, because to him we looked too thin. After we left the pier, he stopped the cab at the first drugstore he could find. He wanted to do something for us as soon as he could to fatten us up a little with something good. He bought me a huge ice cream sundae and Karen a chocolate soda. It was wonderful. We had not had ice cream for so many years, but it also made us very sick. To this day, Karen has not had another chocolate soda. It took a while for us to become accustomed to all the good food in America. As we drove through New York City, on our way to our Onkel Ben and Tante Eldrid's house, we were amazed to see all the food and fruit stands on the sidewalks.

The years following our family's reunion on the dock in New York harbor passed quickly, and now Dad was celebrating his 85th birthday with all of us. It was a milestone he never expected to achieve. And as he enjoyed the Scandinavian treats we made for the special occasion, his mind meandered among the memories he had collected all those years.

He thought of Mom, who had stood by him all this time; and he looked at Karen and me, flashing his patented smile so full of love. Both of us knew he was grateful for the things we had done to make their lives more enjoyable. As we had told them many times, it was a labor of love and a symbol of our appreciation for the sunshine they had brought to our own lives over the years.

We felt so fortunate to have been a part of this family, and to have survived Six Years to Sunrise.

From the Photo Album

Dossi, the elder daughter, was as tall as her mother when Carl met Olga, Karen, and Dossi in New York in November, 1945, after a six-year separation.

In a freedom parade at the end of World War II, Karen was first in line. The date was May 17, 1945.

The German U-boat base as it appears today.

Holen School was rebuilt after the war and looks like this today.

Dossi and Karen with Tore Thomassen (Mossa's husband) in front of Holen School in 1999.

Karen and Catherine return to their wartime home in Laksevåg in 1999.

EPILOGUE

Mom and Dad made one last trip back to Norway in 1981, accompanied by Karen's daughter Jayne (Bannister). Jayne enjoyed traveling with her grandparents and realized, at the conclusion of the trip, that our family's heritage is not only something to talk about, it is an active part of all of our lives. Led by the example of our parents, we have kept our Norwegian heritage alive in the United States.

When Jayne accompanied Mom and Dad during the five week trip, they visited relatives and traveled across the country. It was a rich experience and a dream come true for her. During the trip, she learned about her family's history and some of Norway's history.

She also met relatives that she had known only through photographs and letters up to that point. In addition, she had a chance to walk the streets of Bergen where her Grandparents had been neighbors and later childhood sweethearts.

The most memorable moment of the trip took place on the train ride from Bergen to Oslo, when Mom and Dad held hands as they watched the Norwegian countryside flash by the window of the train. Their love for each other and for their homeland had withstood many challenges over the years, and despite the difficulties they were more in love than ever. To Jayne, this precious instant captured the essence of our family's love for each other and pride in our Norwegian ancestry.

Although we sing Norwegian songs and enjoy our special food selections, our Norwegian ties mean substantially more to us than just that. Our parents taught us the importance and value of carrying on our rich Norwegian traditions and culture, and we're passing along that knowledge to our own children and grandchildren.

We have a lot to be thankful for.

Four generations of the Hoff family in authentic Norwegian dress. From left are Mom (Olga), Karen's daughter Jayne (Bannister), Jessica (Jayne's daughter), and Karen.

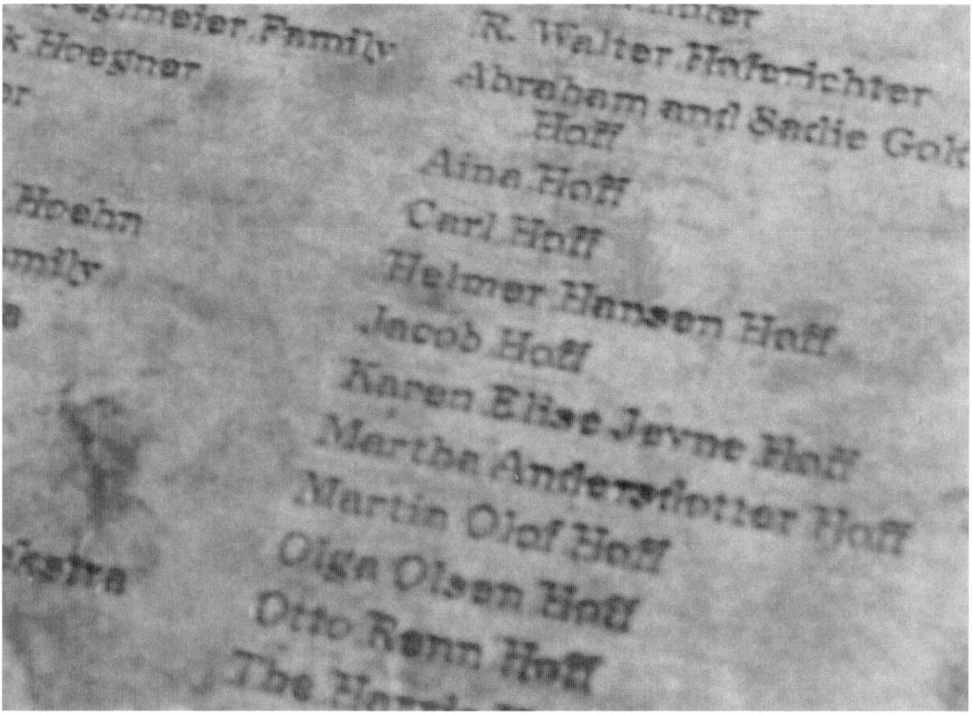

When the Ellis Island restoration project was launched in the 1980's, the Hoff family honored Carl and Olga by arranging for their names to be included on the American Immigrant Wall of Honor. Then they received certificates (shown below) recognizing the importance of their arrivals in America many years before.

ELLIS ISLAND
1892–1992

The Statue of Liberty-Ellis Island Foundation, Inc.
proudly presents this
Official Certificate of Registration
in
THE AMERICAN IMMIGRANT WALL OF HONOR
to officially certify that
CARL HOFF
who came to America from
NORWAY
is among those courageous men and women who came to this country in search of personal freedom, economic opportunity and a future of hope for their families.

Lee A. Iacocca
The Statue of Liberty-Ellis Island Foundation, Inc.

LIBERTY
1886-1986

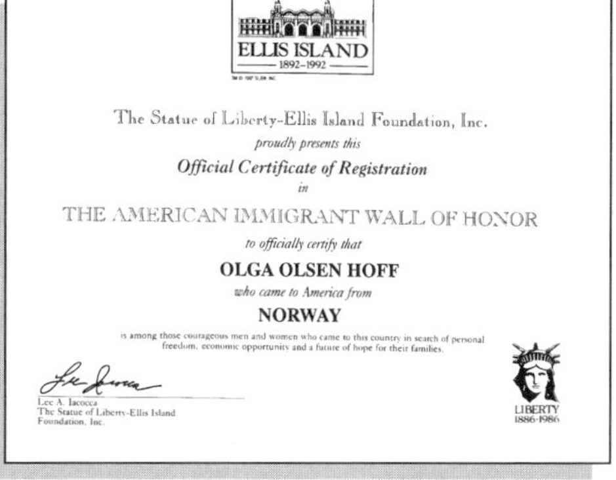

ELLIS ISLAND
1892–1992

The Statue of Liberty-Ellis Island Foundation, Inc.
proudly presents this
Official Certificate of Registration
in
THE AMERICAN IMMIGRANT WALL OF HONOR
to officially certify that
OLGA OLSEN HOFF
who came to America from
NORWAY
is among those courageous men and women who came to this country in search of personal freedom, economic opportunity and a future of hope for their families.

Lee A. Iacocca
The Statue of Liberty-Ellis Island Foundation, Inc.

LIBERTY
1886-1986

ABOUT THE AUTHORS

After Catherine Hoff and Karen Hoff returned from Norway in 1945, they led normal lives once they had readjusted to life in Michigan. Catherine (Dossi) married Clarence Mount, raised two children, and worked for a major international advertising agency in Bloomfield Hills, MI. In recent years, she has worked at a Scandinavian gift shop near her home in Clarkston, MI.

While still in high school, Karen was named Miss Pontiac and the Romeo Peach Queen. She made appearances in parades and other events to promote the two cities. Later, she married Jim Lafnear and together they raised two children. She worked at Pontiac Motors in customer relations and as a bookkeeper for a local oil company.

Olga and Carl Hoff are pictured with their daughters who translated their letters and co-authored Six Years to Sunrise.

Catherine and Karen have made several trips back to Norway, the latest occurring in the summer of 1999.

Harry Knitter was a successful marketing executive with several major firms, including Chrysler and FTD, and he was twice recognized by the American Marketing Association with the presentation of Gold Effie awards for marketing productivity. Since concluding his corporate career, he has written six books and published five. He is president of Kordene Publications, Ltd., a publishing firm which he and his wife, Nancy, formed in 1996.

He has appeared, in behalf of their books, on CNN, The Travel Channel, in the *New York Times*, on PBS, and was interviewed on over 100 local radio and television stations throughout the country.

Harry and Nancy have three sons and live in Clarkston.

Co-Author Harry Knitter has completed six books, all non-fiction.

Kordene Books

Makes Time Fly
When Your Plane Doesn't

HOLDING PATTERN: Airport Waiting Made Easy

by Harry Knitter

Why be discouraged, demoralized, and disappointed when you have to wait for your next flight? This Kordene book will make your waiting time fun and interesting.

The author, a veteran traveler, provides some ingenious ways to pass the time. Also, he rates the top 40 North American airports and describes some of his favorite spots on earth.

$6.95 plus $3.50 S & H
Call 888-567-3363

The Book to Read Before You Book

Why You Should Take Your Travel Agent to Lunch

by Harry Knitter

Your best ally when traveling is your travel agent. The author suggests ways to find a good one, and describes how to capitalize on their knowledge and experience.

He tells why you should avoid booking on the computer and describes several interesting trips he took to Europe. Collaborator William Chiles provides valuable travel agent background.

$6.95 plus $3.50 S & H
Call 888-567-3363

The Book to Save Time and Money While Traveling

101 Stupid Things Business Travelers Do to Sabotage Success

by Harry Knitter

Million-mile traveler and author Harry Knitter tells how to avoid problems and added costs while traveling. Sometimes it just means avoiding an unnecessary trip.

Young business people will find this book an easy way to make trips more productive.

$9.95 plus $3.50 for S & H
Call 888-567-3363

The Flower Book Even Florists Like to Read

A Sweet Sampling of Floral Delights

by Harry Knitter

This is an ideal book for get-well giving, anniversaries, or any special occasions. In prose and poetry, the author covers flower-giving from many perspectives, most of them humorous.

He also includes stories about florists delivering flowers.

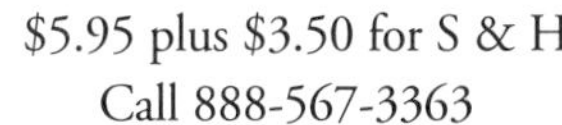
$5.95 plus $3.50 for S & H
Call 888-567-3363

A Smile-Infested Tour of a Great Great Lakes State

The Life & Rhymes of Michigan

by Harry and Nancy Knitter

Fasten your seat belts and hang on to your poetic license. The Knitters take you on a humorous journey you'll thoroughly enjoy.

$6.95 plus $3.50 for S & H
Call 888-567-3363

ORDER FORM

To order additional copies of this book or any other Kordene Publications book (titles below), send your name and shipping address along with a check for the amount of your purchase to: Kordene Publications, P.O. Box 636, Clarkston, MI 48347-0636, or phone: 1-888-567-3363

Name ____

Shipping Address ______________________________

City ________________ State ______ Zip ______________

Book Titles	Price	Quantity
1. *Six Years to Sunrise*	$15.00	______
2. *HOLDING PATTERN: Airport Waiting Made Easy*	$6.95	______
3. *Why You Should Take Your Travel Agent to Lunch*	$6.95	______
4. *101 Stupid Things Business Travelers Do to Sabotage Success*	$9.95	______
5. *A Sweet Sampling of Floral Delights*	$5.95	______
6. *The Life & Rhymes of Michigan*	$6.95	______

Shipping and handling charges (send check with order and save shipping and handling charges):

- $3.50 for one book
- $4.00 for two or three books
- $1.00 each, for orders of four or more books

Michigan residents add 6% sales tax.